THE BIG BOOK OF READING COMPREHENSION ACTIVITIES, GRADE 3

The Big Book of
Reading Comprehension Activities

GRADE 3

100+ Activities for After-School and Summer Reading Fun

By Hannah Braun, MEd

Illustrations by Joel and Ashley Selby

ZEPHYROS
PRESS

Interior and Cover Designer: Michael Cook
Photo Art Director/Art Manager: Sue Bischofberger
Editor: Britt Bogan
Production Editor: Ashley Polikoff
Illustrations © Joel and Ashley Selby

ISBN: Print 978-1-64152-499-5

Contents

Letter to Parents and Teachers vi

100+ Reading Comprehension
Activities 1

Answer Key 112

Skills Index and Common Core
Correlations 118

Letter to Parents and Teachers

Dear parents and teachers,

From the outside, I might have looked like a booklover in high school. I had a checklist of classic novels, and my goal was to read as many of the listed books as I could. Secretly, though, I didn't love books and reading. I was just driven by the idea of testing out of a couple of college classes.

As an adult, I read news articles and books to improve my teaching, but wondered why my friends were so into literature. Reading made-up stories seemed like a waste of time. It's embarrassing to admit that I realized only recently that authors of great literature don't just craft stories; they have something to say about the human condition. Reading through this new lens both expands my thinking and lets me know I'm not alone in my challenges.

I kept this personal breakthrough in mind as I wrote this book. It's important for readers to recall events, understand sequences, and pick out facts. I've included plenty of that kind of practice. Additionally, I've attempted to nudge children toward a love of reading through activities that ask them to look for the author's message and express what it means to them.

This book can be used with child and adult sitting side by side, or with the child working independently and the adult available to answer questions and offer support. Each activity includes a short reading passage, instructions, and an activity to practice a specific skill. The activities get progressively more challenging through the book. You can work through the book sequentially or jump to a specific standard or skill (see the Skills Index and Common Core Correlations on page 118).

I wish you the best of luck as you work toward a deeper understanding of text with your child or student.

Sincerely,
Hannah Braun

100+ Reading Comprehension Activities

LOST AND FOUND

Garrett looked under his bed. He checked behind his door. *Where could they be?* he wondered. Lately, Garrett was having the worst luck with losing things. His watch had gone missing on Monday. On Tuesday he'd lost his light-up pen. Today, he couldn't find his sunglasses. Garrett sighed and left for school without them.

After school, Garrett was watching cartoons. His little brother Isaac was crashing his ride-on toy car into blocks on the floor.

"Hey, Isaac," said Garrett. "Why don't you put those blocks in the trunk of your car?"

"No room," said Isaac. Garrett went over and opened the trunk of the toy car. It was full! Garrett found his watch, pen, and sunglasses inside!

"You're pretty sneaky!" said Garrett.

Isaac giggled.

Complete the crossword puzzle.

1. What is Garrett looking for at the beginning of the story?
2. Garrett says Isaac is sneaky.
3. Who hid Garrett's things?
4. What went missing on Monday?
5. What is Isaac crashing into on the floor?

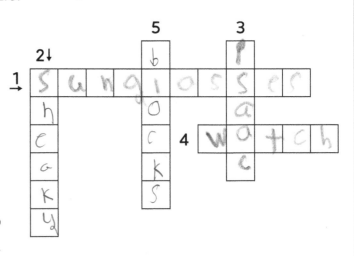

SKILL: Ask and answer questions, referring explicitly to the text

WHAT RED SAID

Emi had just gotten a bird named Red from the pet store.

At home, Red the bird said, "Arf! Arf!" and then, "Meow! Meow!"

"Grandma!" shouted Emi. "Something is wrong with this bird!"

Grandma thought for a minute and then said, "I have an idea. Let's take him to the park." They sat on a bench near trees full of wild birds. Red was watching and listening.

Soon, Red said, "Tweet, tweet! Squawk!"

"I think Red was around the cats and dogs at the pet store for so long that he forgot how to be a bird. Now he remembers!" said Grandma.

Just then, a woman walked by with a barking dog.

"Arf! Arf!" said Red. Grandma and Emi laughed.

Answer the questions below by completing the pictures.

What was the problem in the story?

Red started to say other pet sound instead of speaking what birds usually speak.

How was the problem solved?

grandmas idea worked and was right red wanted to copy the animals because there were his friends in the pet store.

SKILL: Ask and answer questions, referring explicitly to the text

A SHARED LUNCH

Alvaro loved macaroni and cheese. His mom made a variety of other meals, but Alvaro only picked at them.

Alvaro's mom would say, "If you want something else, you'll have to make it yourself." So Alvaro learned how to make macaroni and cheese.

On school days, Alvaro would heat up macaroni and cheese and put it in a thermos so it would still be warm at lunchtime. One morning, Alvaro realized he had forgotten his lunch at home. By lunchtime, Alvaro's stomach was growling.

"Want some grapes?" asked his friend. Alvaro was so hungry that he tried a few. They were sweet and juicy!

"Have some of my turkey sandwich," said another friend. Alvaro liked it. That night at dinner, Alvaro's mom was surprised when he tried everything she made.

Underline the part of the text that answers each question using the color indicated.

1. What did Alvaro use to keep his lunch warm? `Yellow`

   Thermos

2. Why did Alvaro try his friends' food? `Blue`

   he forgot to get his lunch to school

3. Which foods did Alvaro's friends offer him? `Green`

   grapes a turkey sand wich

4. Who was surprised when Alvaro tried new food? `Red`

   alvaros mom

SKILL: Ask and answer questions, referring explicitly to the text

A RACKET ON THE TENNIS COURT

On a summer day, Monica brought a bucket of tennis balls to the park to practice hitting them over the net. She was about to hit the last ball when a group of barking dogs ran onto the court. Each dog scooped up a ball in its mouth. A boy ran up.

"I was helping walk these dogs from the animal shelter, but they got away from me," he said.

The boy crouched low and said, "Come here, doggies!" The dogs also crouched low. He reached out to a dog. It lifted its paw to copy him.

Monica turned around and said, "I can't believe this!" The dogs turned in a circle, too. In frustration, Monica tossed her last ball back into the bucket. The dogs came over and dropped their balls into the bucket. Monica stood, surprised, as the dogs ran off with the boy following them.

Draw a line from a question word to a verb and then to an ending in order to make complete questions. You can use words more than once. Then try to answer the questions.

When	did	the story happen?
Why	were	the dogs run/ running?
Where	did	the dogs give/giving back the balls?

SKILL: Ask and answer questions, referring explicitly to the text

AFTER THE RAIN

One morning, after it had rained all night, I noticed a yellow sign in front of the library. It said, "Closed Due to Flooding." My dad explained that water from the storm had gotten into the library and ruined all the books and furniture. My dad said they would fix it, but it would be a long time before the library was back to normal.

People in town wanted to help. Kids brought in books to donate. The local carpet store gave the library new rugs. A furniture maker donated tables and chairs. An artist painted a new mural inside. When the library opened again, it was full of gifts from everyone in the community. It felt more like our library than ever.

Read the passage to someone else. Then, using a pencil tip, hold the loop of a paper clip to the center of the spinner. Flick the paper clip to spin it. Using the question word on the spinner, ask a question about the text. See if your listener can answer it.

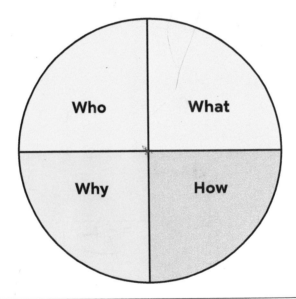

SKILL: Ask and answer questions, referring explicitly to the text

THE BOSSY ROOSTER: A CUBAN FOLKTALE

Rooster was going to a wedding. He stopped to eat some corn and his beak got muddy. Rooster couldn't go to the wedding looking dirty!

He found some grass and said, "Grass, clean off my beak!"

"No!" said the grass.

Rooster said to a goat, "Eat the grass that will not clean my beak!"

"No!" said the goat.

Rooster saw a stick and said, "Stick, hit the goat that will not eat the grass."

"No!" said the stick.

Rooster found some fire and said, "Fire, burn the stick that will not hit the goat."

"I will!" said the fire.

Seeing the fire coming, the stick said, "All right! I'll hit the goat."

The goat got scared and said, "Okay, I'll eat the grass!"

When the grass saw the goat it said, "Wait! I'll clean your beak!"

Rooster made it to the wedding looking very handsome and very clean.

Add words and pictures to the comic strip to retell the story.

FROG'S ESCAPE

Frog was sitting in his favorite spot on the pond, watching the flies buzz around. When one came close, he would snap it up!

Frog noticed a shadow in the tree above him. It was a big snake reaching down to catch him! Frog hopped away. He looked back and saw that the snake was chasing him!

Frog frantically hopped until he got to a different pond and dove into the water. His eyes peered above the surface. There was no sign of the snake. *What bad luck!* thought Frog. *No snack for me and now I'm far away from home!* Frog heard a buzzing sound. All around him were dragonflies that were bigger than any he had seen at his old pond. It had been a scary afternoon, but maybe a juicy snack would come his way after all.

Fill in the blanks to retell the story. Use the shapes to find the letters that will complete the last sentence about the story's lesson.

Frog wanted to catch f l i e s but a s h a k e started chasing him.
　　　　　　　　　　　　　　● 　　　　　　■

He hopped all the way to a different p o n d to escape. Then, he noticed
　　　　　　　　　　　　　　　　　　♥ ↑

there were d r a g o n f i l e s to eat at the new pond.
　　　　　▲ 　★　　　　　　◆

The lesson:
When your plans are r u i n e d, something g o o d can still happen.
　　　　　　　　　　▲ ●■◆↑　　　　　　★♥♥↑

CURTIS'S CUPCAKE

Curtis spent the morning mowing lawns to earn money. He was excited to use some of it to buy a cupcake at the bakery. Curtis took the cupcake home and put it on the counter while he showered.

His sister Tabitha came through the kitchen and ate it. When Curtis found out, he was very angry. Tabitha hadn't realized the cupcake was for Curtis.

The next day, Tabitha said, "Curtis, can you help me get out the hose?" Curtis was still a little angry, but he helped Tabitha anyway. A few hours later, Tabitha came into Curtis's room with a smile on her face and a plate of brownies in her hands. She held it out for Curtis.

"I helped Mrs. Rivera water her flowers and she gave me these. Have some!"

"Thanks, sis!" said Curtis.

If the box shows a person or item from the story, circle the word. Read the circled words from left to right across each line to find out the story's lesson.

find	help	animals	people
even	if	not	they
make	send	you	angry

WAKING UP WALTER

"Wake up, Walter! It's spring!" shouted Ned. Walter snorted, but stayed asleep. Ned crawled into Walter's den.

"Come on, buddy! Hibernation is over. Let's go catch some fish!" said Ned as he shook Walter. Walter just rolled over and kept snoring. *Hmm,* thought Ned. *There's more than one way to wake up a bear!* Ned went home and came back in a couple of hours with a fresh honey cake he had made himself. He put the cake in front of Walter's den and sat on a rock to wait. Soon, Walter appeared, rubbing his eyes.

"I was just dreaming about eating honey cake," yawned Walter. "Hey, where'd this treat come from?"

"I'm glad you're up. Let's go fishing!" said Ned.

"I'm way too hungry for that," said Walter. The bear friends decided to share the cake and go fishing later.

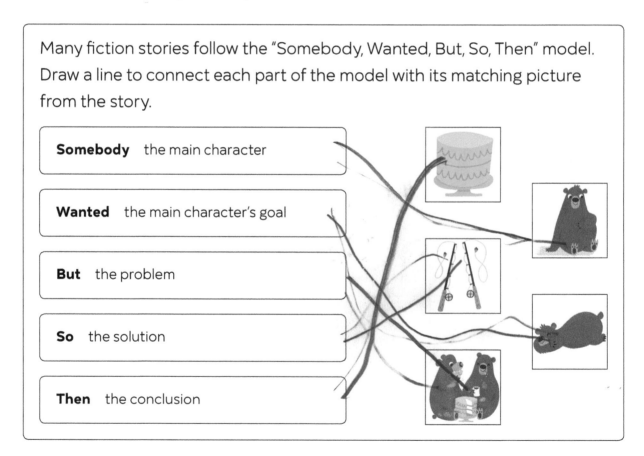

Many fiction stories follow the "Somebody, Wanted, But, So, Then" model. Draw a line to connect each part of the model with its matching picture from the story.

Somebody   the main character

Wanted   the main character's goal

But   the problem

So   the solution

Then   the conclusion

SKILL: Recount stories, determine the central message

HIGH-FLYING IDA

"Ida, you have the biggest teeth I've ever seen!" said Pauline the mouse.

Ida scampered away. She wished her teeth were like the other mice's. Ida looked up and saw a big bunch of balloons tied to a post outside of a store. She climbed the post for a closer look, but got tangled in the strings. While trying to untie herself, she felt her feet lifting off the post. She had untied the balloons from the post, but she was still stuck in them. As she squirmed around, her big teeth slashed against a string and cut it. One balloon floated away and Ida and the other balloons dropped lower. *My teeth!* thought Ida. *That's the answer!* She cut each string with her teeth until there was only one balloon left and she could gently drop to the ground. Ida would never worry about anyone's comments about her teeth again.

Fill in the shapes with the correct words to complete a retelling of the story using the "Somebody, Wanted, But, So, Then" model.

Ida wanted to have **biggest** teeth, but then she got caught up in some **balloons** and floated into the sky.

So she used her big teeth to cut the **strings** and get back to the ground. Then she realized her teeth were useful and she shouldn't **worry** about what other people say.

PERRY'S SURPRISE DISGUISE

Perry's class was putting on a show about famous people. Each student got to choose who they would portray. Perry wanted to surprise his parents, so he wouldn't tell them who he was going to be. His dad liked to make guesses.

"Here's a hint: It's a person who looks a little like me," said Perry.

"You're tall," said his dad. "Is your person a basketball player?"

"Nope!" said Perry.

"You have short brown hair, so maybe you'll be Salvador Dalí, the artist," his dad suggested.

"No way!" said Perry.

"You always wear black. I bet you'll be some kind of government agent," his dad guessed.

On the night of the show, Perry's parents barely recognized him when he came on stage with a tall black hat and a black suit.

Perry announced, "Hello! I'm Abraham Lincoln."

External character traits are details you can see that can be used to describe what a character looks like. Use these details from the text to draw what Perry looks like at his class show.

EVELYN'S ANSWER

Evelyn had been working on her math homework for a while. Her legs were starting to feel restless. Evelyn loved climbing trees, doing cartwheels, and practicing basketball. Sitting quiet and still in a chair was difficult for her. There was only one math problem left, but Evelyn was totally stumped. She tapped her pencil and swung her legs back and forth, but nothing came to her. Evelyn felt like she was going to explode if she had to stare at her math paper for one more minute!

She sprang up and ran out the back door shouting, "Wahoo!"

Evelyn jumped on her trampoline for a while, thinking of nothing but the rhythm of her feet. In midair, she thought, *I've got it!* Evelyn ran back inside and worked out the answer to the last math problem. Taking a break outside was exactly what she needed!

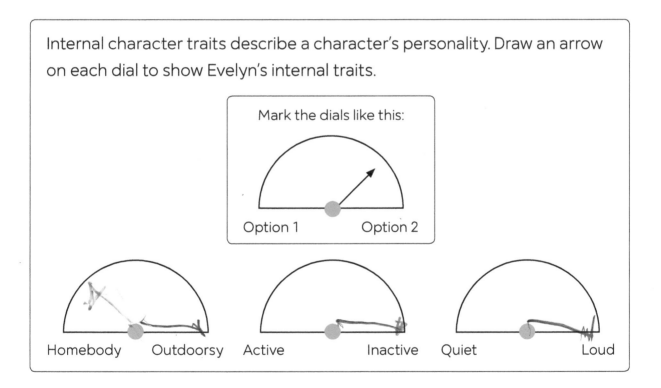

Internal character traits describe a character's personality. Draw an arrow on each dial to show Evelyn's internal traits.

Mark the dials like this:

Option 1   Option 2

Homebody   Outdoorsy   Active   Inactive   Quiet   Loud

SKILL: Describe characters in a story and explain how their actions contribute to the sequence of events

PENGUIN PLUNGE

All the young penguins were learning how to catch fish.

Mr. White, the teacher, demonstrated a graceful dive. The other little penguins dove in, but Raymond laid down and slowly slid from the ice to the water on his belly. It was scary to go in headfirst!

"You've got to dive to be fast enough to catch a fish!" said Mr. White. Raymond felt embarrassed.

On the last day of lessons, Mr. White said, "Class, show me your best dive and you can go out fishing with the big penguins." When it was Raymond's turn, his heart was racing. He closed his eyes, jumped up high, and splashed feetfirst into the water like a cannonball. It was nothing like Mr. White's perfect dive, but the other penguins started cheering. A fish had been thrown out of the water by Raymond's big splash. Raymond was proud. There was more than one way to catch a fish!

Read the statements about the main character's feelings below. If the statement is true, color the check. If the statement is false, color the X.

1. Raymond felt embarrassed because he was smaller than the other penguins. ✓ ⊗
2. Raymond didn't like diving headfirst because it was scary. ✓ ⊗
3. On his final jump, Raymond's heart was probably racing because he felt nervous. ✓ ⊗
4. When the other penguins cheered for Raymond, he felt tired. ✓ ⊗

SKILL: Describe characters in a story and explain how their actions contribute to the sequence of events

INJURY AND INSPIRATION

Angel's class was learning about different careers. When his teacher asked Angel what he wanted to do when he grew up, Angel said, "Can I play video games all day for a job?"

That day after school, Angel was going to try his friend Eli's skateboard.

"Let me show you a few things before you get on," said Eli.

Angel wasn't listening. He pushed off and rolled away.

"You don't know how to turn!" yelled Eli just as Angel got to the end of the street and crashed.

Angel's leg really hurt, so his mom took him to the hospital. He was fascinated by the machines that were used to take X-rays. He asked the staff a lot of questions and looked at the images they took.

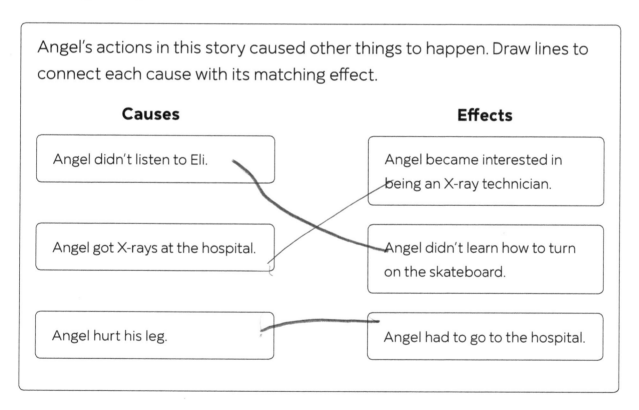

Angel's actions in this story caused other things to happen. Draw lines to connect each cause with its matching effect.

Causes	Effects
Angel didn't listen to Eli.	Angel became interested in being an X-ray technician.
Angel got X-rays at the hospital.	Angel didn't learn how to turn on the skateboard.
Angel hurt his leg.	Angel had to go to the hospital.

SKILL: Describe characters in a story and explain how their actions contribute to the sequence of events

YIKES! SPIDERS!

"Look at this spider I trapped under a glass," said Bryce. "I'm going to take it outside."

"A spider?" asked his brother, Lee. "I'm locking myself in my room where no spiders can get me!"

"Most spiders are harmless," said Bryce. But Lee was headed to his room.

It was a long, lonely day for Lee in his room. When he reached over to turn on his lamp, there was a spider near the switch! Lee ran out of the room.

After he told his mom what happened, she said, "That spider was in your room all day and it didn't do anything to you."

"You're right," said Lee, stopping to think.

"Are you going to find somewhere else to hide out?" asked Lee's mom.

"No," said Lee. "It's not worth it. But can you send Bryce up to catch that spider before I go to bed?"

"I'm on it!" said Bryce.

Write the name of the character that deserves each award based on their traits and actions.

Bravery Around Spiders	Best at Comforting Others	Most Dramatic Reactions
lee	brycee	lee

SKILL: Describe characters in a story and explain how their actions contribute to the sequence of events

A NEW HOME FOR ALVIN

Alvin lived in a cave just like all the other bats. He didn't like the cave, but, being a bat, he had no other choice.

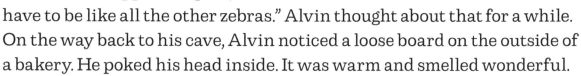

One day, Ursula the zebra caught his eye. She was wearing a shirt covered in black and white dots.

"Ursula, why are you wearing that shirt? Zebras are known for their stripes!" said Alvin.

"I'm much happier in spots," said Ursula. "I don't have to be like all the other zebras." Alvin thought about that for a while. On the way back to his cave, Alvin noticed a loose board on the outside of a bakery. He poked his head inside. It was warm and smelled wonderful.

Another bat saw him and said, "What are you doing? It's time to go back to the cave."

Alvin called back, "I'm trying something new today." He found a rafter and slept more comfortably than ever before.

Using details from the picture, find and circle the words in the word search that describe the cave. There are seven words to find.

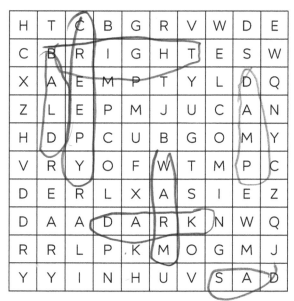

H	T	C	B	G	R	V	W	D	E
C	B	R	I	G	H	T	E	S	W
X	A	E	M	P	T	Y	L	D	Q
Z	L	E	P	M	J	U	C	A	N
H	D	P	C	U	B	G	O	M	Y
V	R	Y	O	F	W	T	M	P	C
D	E	R	L	X	A	S	I	E	Z
D	A	A	D	A	R	K	N	W	Q
R	R	L	P	K	M	O	G	M	J
Y	Y	I	N	H	U	V	S	A	D

SKILL: Explain how text's illustrations contribute to what is conveyed by the words

HELP IN THE STORM

Claire and her family were moving to a new home out west with many other families. One cloudy evening, the group was setting up camp. Claire's dad asked her to fill their bucket with water from a stream. She was glad for a reason to get away from Elijah, a boy from the group who had been annoying her with silly jokes for days. When she got to the stream, heavy rain started falling. Claire was alone and afraid.

She heard a voice shout, "Over here!" Claire ran up the creek to an old wagon that was overturned. Inside was Elijah. She never thought she'd be so happy to see him! They waited out the storm and headed back to the camp as the clouds cleared. It was hard to get along with Elijah, but Claire appreciated his help and vowed to help him when he needed it.

Mark on the picture according to the following statements:

1. Draw an arrow to something that tells you this story happened in the past.

2. Draw a star next to something that tells you this picture is from the end of the story.

3. Draw a box around the part of the picture that tells you the story is happening far away from any city.

4. Draw a circle around something Claire's bucket of water might have been used for.

SKILL: Explain how text's illustrations contribute to what is conveyed by the words

SPRING BREAK PLANS

"I'm spending all of spring break at the beach," announced Rachel. "What about you?"

"I've got a big trip planned," said Taylor. "My plane leaves tomorrow."

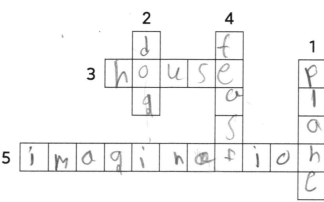

The next day, Taylor boarded her plane and set off for a spring break adventure. She landed in a familiar place. Taylor went outside and was nearly plowed over by a beast with a wagging tail and a wet nose. She tamed the beast and they explored the landscape together. Soon, Taylor's mom brought her something to eat.

"Oh, thank you!" said Taylor. "A feast! I do love to sample the local specialties on my travels." Taylor's mom laughed and went back inside.

Back at school the following week, Taylor sat next to Rachel at lunch.

"Well, how was your trip? What did you do? Tell me all about it," said Rachel.

"You'll just have to use your imagination," said Taylor with a smile.

Use information from the text and the illustration to complete the crossword puzzle.

1. Taylor flies on a pretend plane.
2. The beast she finds is really a dog.
3. The landscape she explores is outside of her house.
4. When Taylor's mom brings her a snack, she sees it as a feast.
5. Taylor uses her imagination to make her spring break trip happen.

Crossword answers:
- 3 across: house
- 2 down: dog
- 4 down: feast
- 5 across: imagination
- 1 down: plane

KELTON'S EXPERIMENT

Kelton's mom walked into the kitchen. She could see that Kelton had been very busy.

"I'm trying to do a cool experiment that I saw on a science show. I mixed a few ingredients from your baking supplies together, but nothing's happening," he said.

"I've got a science experiment that you can help me with," said Kelton's mom. She took him over to a pan that was very dirty from cooking dinner. "Scrub this with baking soda first." Kelton scrubbed until most of the grime was loose. "Now rinse it off with some vinegar." Kelton poured some vinegar in the pan and everything started bubbling!

"That's a great science experiment, Mom!" said Kelton, but his mom was gathering an armload of dishes for him. It looked like Kelton would be busy for a while!

Use the picture to imagine how Kelton's mom feels in this situation. Fill in the blanks to show what she might be thinking.

I am _sady_ to see that this kitchen is so _dirty_. What is _Kelton_ trying to do in here? I'll try to get him to help _clean_ the _kitchen_

SKILL: Explain how text's illustrations contribute to what is conveyed by the words

WALKING ON THE MOON

In 1969, three astronauts took a trip to the moon. After three days of space travel, they arrived. The main spacecraft, called the control module, didn't land on the moon. It orbited around the moon. A smaller vehicle, called the lunar module, was sent down to the surface of the moon with two astronauts inside. The third astronaut remained in the control module.

On the moon, the two astronauts collected samples and explored. They left a few things behind, like the United States' flag and a sign to say who had been there. They also left their footprints. Today, the footprints are still on the dusty surface of the moon because there is no wind, water, or living things to disturb them. The first moon landing was an incredible scientific accomplishment for humans.

There is something wrong in each statement below. Cross out the errors and write in your corrections.

1. ~~The main spacecraft was called the rocket.~~

2. ~~The astronauts left their boots on the moon.~~

3. There were six astronauts on the first trip to the moon.

4. It took three hours to get from Earth to the moon.

SKILL: Ask and answer questions to demonstrate understanding of a text, referring explicitly to the text

HOW THE HIPPO GOT ITS NAME

The word "hippopotamus" was made up by the ancient Greeks. When the Greeks saw this unfamiliar animal while traveling in Africa, they thought it looked like a river horse! In the Greek language, "hippo" means horse, and "potamos" means river. Hippos and horses do have some similar characteristics. Both have long heads with their ears, eyes, and nostrils near the top. Both animals also eat grass.

However, hippos and horses have very different behavior. Hippos spend most of the day in the water. They venture on land at night to eat grass. While horses can swim, they rarely go in water. Horses, with their long legs and lean bodies, can run much faster than hippos. Horses and hippos are not closely related, but it's easy to spot the similarities that the ancient Greeks probably noticed.

Answer the questions below by marking parts of the text in the color indicated.

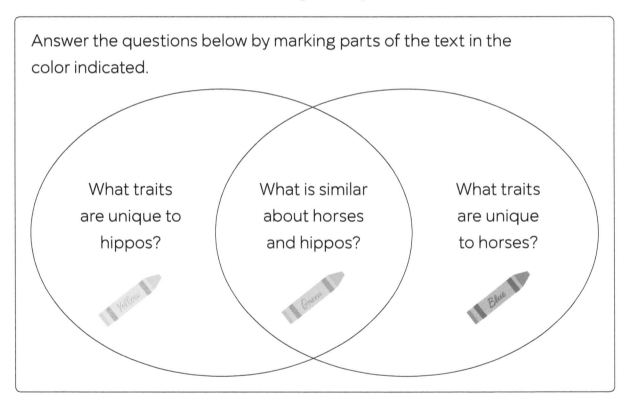

What traits are unique to hippos?

What is similar about horses and hippos?

What traits are unique to horses?

SKILL: Ask and answer questions to demonstrate understanding of a text, referring explicitly to the text

CELEBRATING HOLI

At the end of winter, many people in India celebrate Holi. The night before Holi, people light bonfires that represent the triumph of good over evil. People gather around the bonfires to sing and dance.

The next day, people throw colored powder on each other in a friendly free-for-all. This is why Holi is also known as the Festival of Colors. After a day of covering neighbors and strangers in color, people clean up before visiting family and friends. They share special foods together.

Holi is seen as a time of new beginnings. A new growing season is starting. People are encouraged to let go of old arguments and renew friendships. Indians kick off spring in a colorful way by celebrating Holi.

Fill in the blanks with information from the text. Then, use the shapes to find the letters that complete the last sentence.

1. Another name for Holi is the Festival of _lights_.
   ▲

2. Holi is from the country _India_.
   ★ ♥

3. People celebrate by dancing and singing around _bonfires_.
   ◆ ●

4. People throw colored _Power_ on each other.
   ■

In ancient India, _anyone_ could throw powder at the
♥ ★ ◆ ★ ●

Cmpetot during Holi.
● ■ ● ▲ ◆ ▲

ROCK ART

Long ago, before people wrote on paper, they left marks by picking, cutting, or scratching on rocks with stone tools. When the outer surface of the rock was scratched away, a different color of rock was revealed underneath. These marks are called petroglyphs. In places where rocks stay dry and protected, petroglyphs can still be seen today.

Petroglyphs show a wide variety of images. Some petroglyphs show recognizable animals like horses or sheep. Others show people, handprints, and shapes. They may have been carved to record stories, create maps, or mark the movement of the stars. Petroglyphs give modern people clues about how prehistoric people lived. It's important to only look at or photograph petroglyphs and not touch them. This way, people for years to come can enjoy and learn from them.

Draw lines from a question word, to a verb, and then to an ending in order to make complete questions. You can use words more than once. Then try to find the answers.

How	were	petroglyphs made?
What	are	petroglyphs?
Why	can	we learn from petroglyphs?

SKILL: Ask and answer questions to demonstrate understanding of a text, referring explicitly to the text

FROM SEED TO CHRISTMAS TREE

Plants that people use for food are grown on farms. You might be surprised to learn that there are also farms for Christmas trees. At these farms, tree seeds are planted in trays and cared for in greenhouses. When the new trees are big enough, they are planted in the ground outside. It takes about six years for a new tree to grow big enough to become a Christmas tree.

Before Christmas, farm workers cut down the biggest trees with chain saws. At some farms, workers bundle up several cut trees and then use a helicopter to pick up the bundles and move them to big trucks. The trees are then sent all over the world to be decorated for Christmas.

Read the statements about Christmas tree farming. If the statement is true, color the check. If the statement is false, color the X.

1. After two years, a new tree grows big enough to be a Christmas tree.

2. Some Christmas tree farms use helicopters to move cut trees around.

3. Seeds for new trees are first planted in the ground.

4. Farm workers pull the trees up from their roots to harvest them.

SKILL: Ask and answer questions to demonstrate understanding of a text, referring explicitly to the text

THE LIVES OF CAMELS

☐ **Thriving in the Desert**
Camels live in deserts, which are hot and dry. Camels have special features that help them survive in this harsh environment. They have bushy eyebrows to keep sand out of their eyes. They have wide feet to keep them from sinking into the sand.

☐ **Diet**
Some camels are cared for by people. People feed camels grass and grains like oats. Camels living on their own will eat any plant matter they can find, including leaves, twigs, and seeds.

☐ **Camels and People**
People use camels for riding on and for carrying things. Camels can also provide meat, milk, and wool.

The bold words at the beginning of each section are called headings. Headings tell you what a section of text will be about. Each sentence below was left out of the text. Draw the sentence's symbol in the box for the section where it fits best.

 When camels are doing jobs for people, they are called domesticated camels.

 Camels have rough patches on their knees that protect them when kneeling on hot sand.

 Camels are even known to eat leather or their owner's tents when there isn't much regular food.

SKILL: Use text features to locate information efficiently

TAKING A CAMPING TRIP

TABLE OF CONTENTS

Chapter 1: Equipment 3
Making Shelter 4
Outdoor Clothing 8
Wood Gathering Tools 13

Chapter 2: Cooking Outdoors 14
Cooking Over a Fire 15
Using a Propane Stove 17
Keeping Food Cold 20
Recipes 21

Chapter 3: Safety 35
Preparing a First-Aid Kit 36
Fire Safety 39
Encountering Wildlife 41

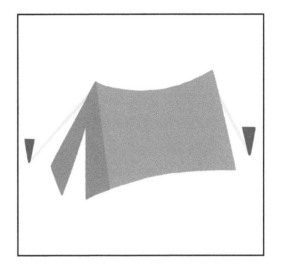

This is the table of contents from a book about camping. Circle the part of the table of contents where you could find the answer to each question below. Use the colors indicated.

Where would you look to find . . .

1. what to do if you saw a bear?   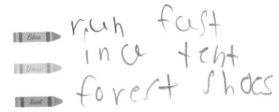 Blue

2. something to make for breakfast?   Green

3. what kind of shoes to wear?   Red

4. information about tents?   Yellow

(handwritten: run fast in a tent forest shoes)

SKILL: Use text features to locate information efficiently

RESCUING BABY ELEPHANTS

Just like human babies, baby elephants need to be cared for. Sometimes an elephant mother dies or gets separated from her baby. When this happens, elephant rescuers in Kenya help out.

Orphaned baby elephants are brought to a nursery where they are fed and kept safe. The youngest elephants are fed with big bottles but soon learn to find their own food. The young elephants enjoy playing with each other, spraying water, and rolling in the mud to stay cool.

Baby elephants enjoy kicking a soccer ball at the nursery.

After about three years, workers release the elephants into wildlife parks around Kenya so that they can stay wild.

Pictures and captions can tell you more about the topic of the text. Use the text, picture, and caption to fill in the word shapes below.

1. Orphaned baby elephants eat from  b o t t l e s .

2. The elephants have fun kicking a s o c c e r b a l l

   and rolling in the  m u d .

3. An elephant will stay at the nursery for about t h r e e

    y e a r s .

4. When they grow big enough, they are released to a

   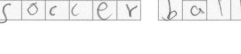 w i l d l i f e park.

SKILL: Use text features to locate information efficiently

THE RISE OF THE ROLLER COASTER

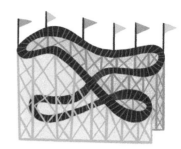

The first roller coasters were hills of ice and snow in Russia. People sledded down the hills for fun. The first modern roller coaster with wheeled cars secured to a track was built in France. In the United States, mining companies **imitated** this idea by selling rides on their downhill rail lines to thrill-seekers. Soon, builders were making roller coasters with dark tunnels and painted scenery.

Disneyland hugely improved roller coaster construction when it built a track made from steel tubes instead of wood. Steel tracks can be bent in any direction, which allows designers to add loops and **corkscrews** to roller coaster rides. Many of the newest roller coasters change the position of the rider. Instead of facing forward, riders can stand, be **suspended**, or lay in a flying position. Roller coasters are a **staple** of modern amusement parks.

Glossary

corkscrew – a spiral shape
imitated – copied

staple – an important part
suspended – hanging

A glossary defines words in a text that you might not know. Use the glossary to complete the crossword puzzle.

1. a spiral shape
2. something essential
3. a bird feeder is often _ _ _ _ _ _ _ _ _ from a branch
4. did the same as

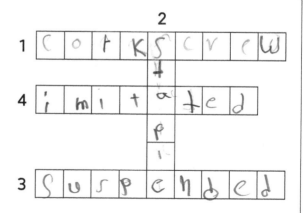

BECOMING A BUTTERFLY

Most babies look like their parents, only smaller. However, butterfly babies don't look like their parents at all. There are four stages in a butterfly's life cycle. They start their lives in the egg stage. After the egg hatches, the larva stage begins. The larva, or caterpillar, eats and grows quickly. It will shed its skin as it gets bigger.

When the larva is done growing, it enters the pupa stage. In this stage, the larva attaches itself to a branch and sheds its skin one last time to reveal a chrysalis. Th chrysalis protects the insect while it changes inside. Inside the chrysalis, the insect's cells break down and reform in a new way. Later, a butterfly emerges from the chrysalis. This is the adult stage. Adult females can lay eggs and start the process over again.

Use information from the text to label each stage in the butterfly life cycle.

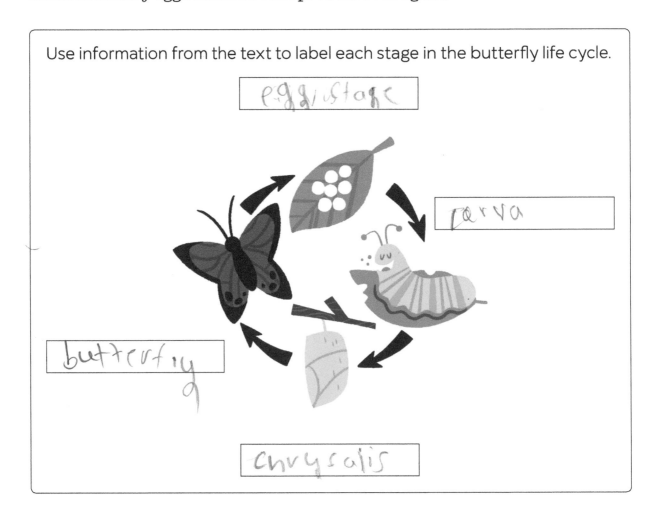

egg stage

larva

butterfly

chrysalis

SKILL: Use information gained from illustrations and the words to demonstrate understanding of the text

HOW TO DRAW A BIRD

Drawing doesn't have to be complicated. Even professional artists start their work by drawing simple lines and shapes. You can use lines and shapes to draw a bird.

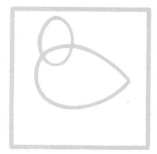

First, draw a circle for the head. Then add an oval for the body, and a thin rectangle for the tail.

Next, draw a curve on the body to show the location of the wing. Draw a triangle on the head for the beak.

Finally, add details like feathers, eyes, and feet. You can even add a background to show where your bird lives.

Read the directions and use the pictures to draw your own bird in the frame below.

SKILL: Use information gained from illustrations and the words to demonstrate understanding of the text

A MUSEUM TRIP

Dear Museum Staff,

I am visiting your museum next week with my five-year-old son. I need your help to plan our trip. We will be at the museum long enough to see four exhibits. We know that we don't want to see the mummies because my son is scared of them. However, he loves dinosaurs and is excited to see your fossil displays. Also, at some point in our trip we will need to stop for a snack. Can you help us plan out the path we should take through the museum? We would like to spend lots of time looking at exhibits, not walking back and forth.

Sincerely,
Mrs. Guzman

Mark the path that Mrs. Guzman and her son should take through the museum on their trip. Start at the lobby. Can you plan a trip that matches all of her requests?

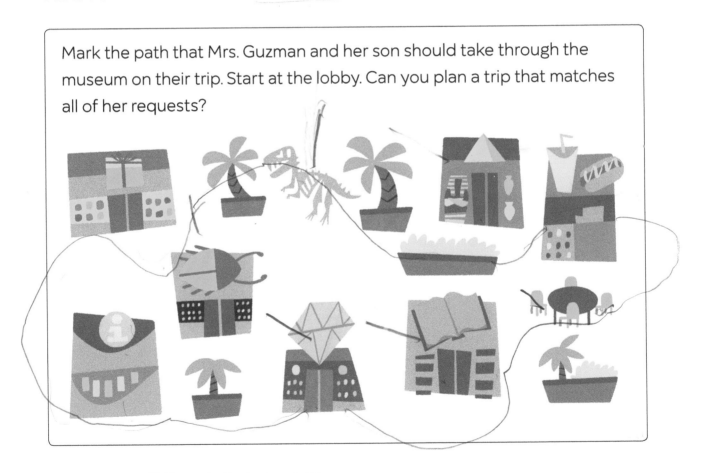

SKILL: Use information gained from illustrations and the words to demonstrate understanding of the text

ANIMAL LONG JUMPERS

Animals have special skills to help them survive in their habitats. Some animals are excellent jumpers.

  Kangaroos, with their strong legs, are known for jumping. They can cover up to 25 feet in a single bound. Jumping so far helps them cover long distances in search of food and water. Mountain goats need to move across steep terrain. They can jump distances of 13 feet. Living high in the mountains keeps them away from predators. Impalas are a kind of antelope that lives in Africa. They run and jump to escape predators. Impalas can jump 33 feet in a single leap.

  For comparison, the average human can make a long jump of about 7 feet. Animals built for jumping can cover impressive distances.

Use the text and the graph to answer the questions below.

1. Which animal jumps the farthest? _Impala_

2. Which animal jumps about twice as far as a mountain goat? _kangaroo_

3. Which animal jumps to search for food and water? _kangaroo_

4. The shortest jumper is the _human_.

SKILL: Use information gained from illustrations and the words to demonstrate understanding of the text

CHUCK WHAT?

If there was an award for the funniest animal name, the chuckwalla might win. Chuckwallas are lizards that live in the southwestern United States. They have wide bodies and thick tails. Chuckwallas can grow to be about 15 inches long. They are harmless to humans and like to eat leaves, fruit, and flowers. They get almost all of the water they need from the plant material that they eat. Chuckwallas are ectothermic, which means they don't make much of their own body heat. They bask in the sun to warm up. During the colder months, chuckwallas hibernate. When a chuckwalla senses danger, it hides between rocks. They prefer to live in rocky areas. The desert survival ability of the chuckwalla is no joke.

Find things in the word search that a chuckwalla would have in its habitat. Use clues from the text and the picture. There are seven words to find.

Q	A	L	E	A	V	E	S	Z	W
S	X	E	D	C	R	F	V	T	G
B	Y	H	F	N	F	R	U	I	T
U	C	J	L	M	I	O	K	O	L
P	A	Q	O	A	Z	C	W	S	X
E	C	D	W	C	R	K	F	V	T
G	T	B	E	Y	H	S	A	N	D
N	U	J	R	M	U	I	K	O	L
P	S	Q	S	A	Z	W	S	X	E
D	C	H	E	A	T	R	F	V	T

SKILL: Use information gained from illustrations and the words to demonstrate understanding of the text

WORKING AS A VETERINARIAN

Before you read, it's helpful to think about what you already know about the topic. Then you can connect new information to what you already know. This text is about veterinarians, who are also called vets. Using the checklist below, check off anything that you already know or have experienced about veterinarians.

☐ I have taken a pet to the vet.

☑ I have seen a vet on TV.

☐ I have helped take care of an animal.

Veterinarians are doctors for animals. They have to enjoy working with many kinds of animals, even rats and snakes. In addition to caring for pets, vets can take care of zoo animals or farm animals. People that want to become vets have to go to college and study veterinary medicine. They will take a lot of math and science classes. After college, they have to go to vet school for four more years. Finally, after a year of on-the-job training, they can become a doctor of veterinary medicine.

Some of the challenges of being a vet are working with aggressive or scared animals and working unusual hours. However, vets enjoy the reward of helping animals stay healthy.

Considering what you already know and using the information in the text, would you like to work as a vet? Talk about it with your parent, a teacher, or a friend.

SKILL: Activate prior knowledge

ROCKS: FROM SOLID TO LIQUID

Think of things you already know about rocks and magma. Write them in the "Before Reading" column of the chart below. After reading, see if there's anything new you learned that you can add to the in the "After Reading" column of chart.

Before Reading	After Reading
Rocks A rock is a solid thing that we can see outside	**Rocks** Can melt and become liquids burried deep inside the earth
Magma magma can form into a volcano erupting	**Magma** is a thick layer of a liquid rock. Magma that comes out from a volcano is called lava.

When you hold a solid rock in your hand, it's hard to imagine that it could ever become liquid. However, when rocks are buried deep inside the Earth, heat and pressure make them melt. Many miles under your feet, there is a thick layer of liquid rock called magma. Most of the time magma stays deep within the Earth, but sometimes it pushes its way to the surface. When this happens, a volcano forms. Magma that comes out of a volcano is called lava.

When lava is exposed to the air it begins to cool down and become solid rock again. This is similar to how candle wax is a liquid when it's near a flame but cools down and gets hard again when the flame is blown out. After thousands of years, the newly formed rock may get buried and melted and the cycle will repeat.

SKILL: Activate prior knowledge

WHY WE SLEEP

Scientists don't know exactly why we sleep, but they have a few ideas. Sleeping helps reset our bodies and brains. When we are awake, the cells in our brains make chemicals that build up and make us feel tired. When we sleep, the body clears away these chemicals. Our bodies also get a chance to heal and repair themselves while we sleep. When people are sick, they tend to sleep more so their body can heal.

Sleep is also connected to learning. When people learn things, they make new connections in their brains. Those brain connections seem to be strengthened during sleep. People who don't get enough sleep have trouble remembering things they've learned. Babies learn new things all the time, so they need a lot of sleep. Humans definitely perform better with enough sleep.

We can understand what we read better when we connect it to our own lives and the world around us. Talk to someone else about this passage. Check off a trophy for each question you can answer or each sentence you can complete.

☑ What do you notice about your sleep habits when you're sick?

☑ What do you notice about babies and sleep?

☑ One time when I didn't sleep enough, I felt tired

SKILL: Make connections to self and the world

FROM OLD PAPER TO NEW

Paper is made from trees. When used paper gets recycled, fewer trees have to be cut down. Making new paper from old paper also saves water, electricity, and space in landfills. Here's how it works:

Used paper is taken to a paper mill. There, it is shredded into small pieces. The paper pieces are mixed with water and chemicals to break them down into fibers. The mixture is pressed through a screen to remove staples and then spun in a cone-shaped container to remove ink and glue. Next, the mixture is sprayed onto a conveyer belt. Water from the mixture drips through the belt and the paper fibers start bonding together again. Then, heated metal rollers dry and flatten the paper into big rolls. The rolls can be made into new paper products.

Use pictures or words to respond to each prompt.

A container I have seen to collect used paper:

A way I have reused paper:

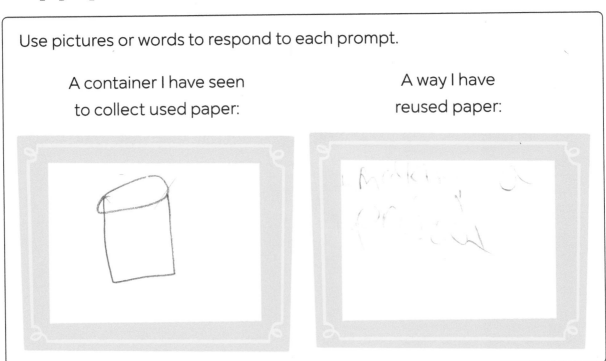

SKILL: Make connections to self and the world

OH, DEER!

A little deer was walking in the woods with his mom. He stopped at a stream for a drink. When he looked up, he couldn't see his mom anymore. He heard a rustle in the trees and followed it, trying to catch up. Soon he turned a corner and saw that he had actually been following a skunk!

What do you think will happen next? Write your prediction in the space, then keep reading.

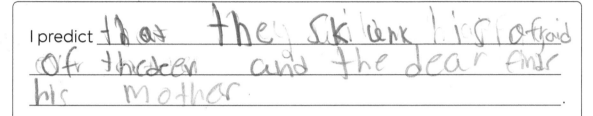

I predict _that they skunk lisi afraid ofr thedeer and the dear fmar his mothar_.

Read the passage below. If your prediction was right, color in the check mark. If you had to change your thinking, color in the X. It's okay to change your thinking. Good readers do it all the time.

Check your prediction.

The little deer turned to run away. Then, he realized that the skunk was actually more afraid of him. The skunk climbed straight up the nearest tree, screeching all the way. By the time it got to the top of the tree, the skunk's noises had carried through the forest. The mother deer heard the commotion and came running to see what was happening. There she found the little deer, staring up at the tree. The deer went on their way, keeping a more careful eye on each other.

SKILL: Ask and answer questions, referring explicitly to the text

A GOOD START

Sometimes an author doesn't explain exactly what happened in a story. You have to use what you already know, along with clues the author gives you, to figure it out. This is called making an inference. Read each section of the story. Then color the smiley face next to the inference that matches the clues the author gave.

Story	Inferences
Kristen was waiting at the bus stop. She was going to a new school this year. It felt like she had butterflies in her stomach.	☺ Kristen feels tired. ☺ Kristen feels nervous.
She had never ridden a school bus. How would she know where to get off at the end of the day? She noticed a boy frantically looking through his backpack. He looked worried.	☺ The boy is missing something. ☺ The boy likes his backpack.
"What's going on?" Kristen asked him. "I think I left my lunch at home," said the boy. His shoulders slumped.	☺ The boy feels sad. ☺ The boy's shoulder muscles are sore.

Kristin opened her backpack. "Here," she said. "This was my snack for the ride home, but you can have it."

The boy's face lit up. "Thank you! I'll bring a snack to pay you back tomorrow," he said.

"I've got a better way for you to pay me back," said Kristin. "Help me know when to get off the bus on the ride home."

They gave each other a high five as the bus was pulling up at school.

SKILL: Ask and answer questions, referring explicitly to the text

THE TRUE STORY OF CINDERELLA

If you've heard the story of Cinderella, you've been lied to! Take it from me, Cinderella's stepsister. I know what really happened.

The day of the ball, my mom told us that we had to finish our chores before we went. All Cinderella did was sit on the floor with a scrub brush and sing! When it was time to leave for the palace, she had to stay behind.

Surprisingly, I saw her at the palace later! She must have snuck away from home and stolen shoes and a dress on the way.

The next day, the prince came to our house with one of the shoes she had been wearing. I tried it on, hoping to return it to the store. When the shoe slipped easily onto Cinderella's foot, the prince said he would marry her! The king had better hide his crown before Cinderella moves in and steals that, too!

Complete the crossword puzzle using the missing words from the sentences below.

1. Cinderella was supposed to finish her _Chores_ before the ball.
2. Cinderella's _stepsister_ is telling the story.
3. The narrator says Cinderella _stole_ a dress and shoes.
4. The narrator wanted to _return_ the shoe to the store.

Crossword:
- 1 ACROSS: C H O R E S
- 4 DOWN: (r) e t u r n
- 2 DOWN: (s) t e p s i s t e r
- 3 ACROSS: S T O L E

SKILL: Ask and answer questions, referring explicitly to the text

TAKING CARE OF ALYSSA

Matthew noticed that every morning Alyssa got each person at the table a sharp pencil. If anyone felt left out at recess, Alyssa asked them to play with her. During math, she patiently explained how she got her answers if someone didn't understand.

One morning, Alyssa didn't sharpen the pencils. She sat with her head down on her desk. When Matthew asked her what was wrong, Alyssa mumbled that her head hurt. At recess, Alyssa didn't feel like playing so she went to the nurse.

Later, Alyssa walked back into class and sadly said, "Mr. Florian, I have to go home. I'm sick." Right away Matthew thought, *What would Alyssa do for me if I was sick?* He made sure Alyssa had all of her things.

He told her, "Don't worry about your writing materials. I'll clean them up." Then he patiently walked with her down to the office to wait for her mom.

If the statement is true, color the check. If the statement is false, color the X.

1. Matthew always got sharp pencils for his table group.
2. Matthew has learned how to care for others by watching Alyssa.
3. Alyssa missed recess to help clean the classroom.
4. Mr. Florian is the school nurse.

SKILL: Ask and answer questions, referring explicitly to the text

HURRY UP, HENRY!

One day, Mother Gorilla returned to her leaf nest and found two babies in it instead of one! She cared for the extra baby as her own and called him Henry.

Henry walked slowly, ate slowly, and was always the last to climb into the leaf nest to sleep. He felt like he didn't fit in with the other gorillas. Mother Gorilla was always saying, "Hurry up, Henry!"

One day, a strange animal with long arms and legs slowly climbed down one of the trees where the gorillas lived.

"Oh, there you are!" said the animal. "I've been climbing around this tree for days looking for you!"

"Who are you?" asked Henry.

"Don't be silly. I'm your mom! Thanks for looking out for my baby, Mother Gorilla. I'll carry him back up to the other sloths now." *Sloths?* thought Henry. Henry soon found a community that was much more his speed and he knew he was home.

Read the passage to someone else. Then, using a pencil tip, hold the loop of a paper clip to the center of the spinner. Flick the paper clip to spin it. Using the question word on the spinner, ask a question about the text. See if your listener can answer it.

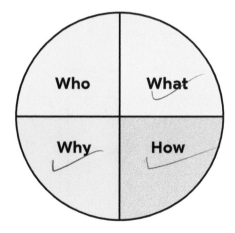

SKILL: Ask and answer questions, referring explicitly to the text

THE CLEVER BEETLE

One morning, Enrique the beetle set out to meet his beetle friend who lived near the top of a tree. Enrique had started climbing up the trunk when he noticed a bird pecking at things on the ground. The bird looked hungry, so Enrique quickly went around to the back side of the tree and kept climbing. He thought he was safe, but suddenly the bird perched on a branch beside him.

"Hello, little beetle," said the bird. "Where are you headed?"

"I'm meeting my friend higher up in this tree," said Enrique.

"Two beetles! What a lucky day for me," said the hungry bird. Enrique thought quickly.

"Oh no, my friend is a ... a snake!" Enrique said. "His favorite food is bird pudding." Startled, the bird fluttered its feathers, chirped, and flew away. Enrique made his way up the tree and enjoyed the day with his friend.

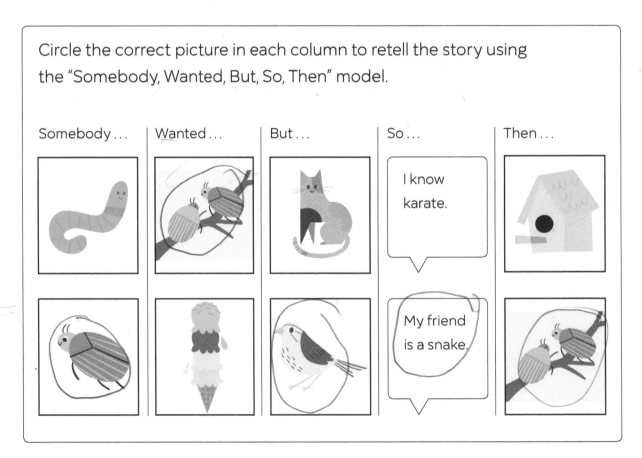

Circle the correct picture in each column to retell the story using the "Somebody, Wanted, But, So, Then" model.

SKILL: Recount stories, determine the central message

THESEUS AND THE MINOTAUR: A MYTH

Long ago, a king named Minos had a creature with the head of a bull and the body of a human. It was called a Minotaur. King Minos kept the Minotaur in an underground labyrinth, or maze. Once a year, the king sent a group of people from Athens, an enemy city, into the labyrinth to be eaten by the Minotaur.

The king of Athens had a son named Theseus. One year, Theseus volunteered to go into the labyrinth. He planned to kill the Minotaur so that no more of his countrymen could be eaten. Before entering the labyrinth, Theseus met King Minos's daughter. She gave Theseus string to unravel as he went through the maze.

Theseus battled and killed the Minotaur. Then he followed the string to find his way back out of the labyrinth. Theseus became a hero in Athens.

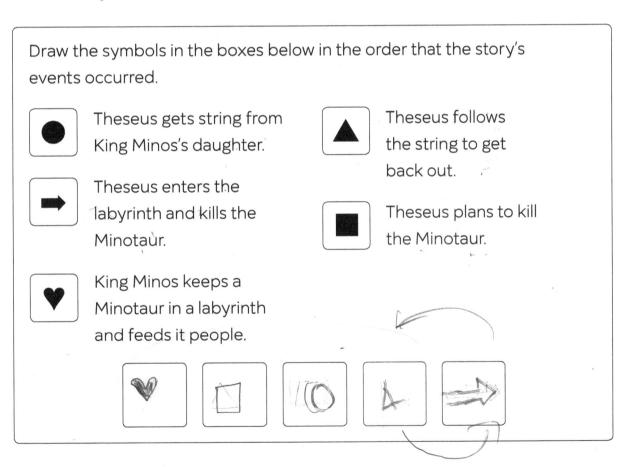

Draw the symbols in the boxes below in the order that the story's events occurred.

● Theseus gets string from King Minos's daughter.

▲ Theseus follows the string to get back out.

➡ Theseus enters the labyrinth and kills the Minotaur.

■ Theseus plans to kill the Minotaur.

♥ King Minos keeps a Minotaur in a labyrinth and feeds it people.

SKILL: Recount stories, determine the central message

PAUL'S REPORT

Paul and his mom were at a park walking along a stream.

"What's wrong?" asked Paul's mom.

"I have to give my report in front of the class tomorrow. Last time I talked in front of the class, my throat felt tight and my voice was wobbly," said Paul. "I wish I were braver."

"When you're brave, it means you feel afraid but you do what needs to be done anyway," said Paul's mom. She picked up a smooth stone and pressed it into Paul's hand. "Put this in your pocket tomorrow to remind you that I'm thinking of you and I know you can do it."

The next day, Paul stood up in front of the class. His stomach was churning. He put his hand in his pocket and touched the smooth stone. Paul took a deep breath and, although he was a little scared, he bravely gave his report. At the end, everyone clapped.

Fill in the blanks with information from the text. Then, use the shapes to find the letters that complete the last sentence.

1. Paul is worried about giving a _report_.
   ★

2. He wants to feel _brave_ but thinks his voice will be _wobbly_.
   ♥ ■   ●

3. His mom gives him a _stone_ so he'll know that she's
   ▲

   thinking of him.
   ◆

Paul learned that you can be both _afraid_ and _brave_ at the same time.
♥   ★ ♥ ◆   ● ★ ♥ ■ ▲

SKILL: Recount stories, determine the central message

JADA'S PAINT BOX

Jada had a special box of paints. When she used them, she was very careful to never mix the colors or drip paint outside of the circles. One day, Jada was painting when the doorbell rang. Jada's mom answered it and in walked Amanda, Jada's friend.

"You're painting? I love painting!" said Amanda. "Can I do it, too?"

"No," said Jada. "These are my special paints. I don't want them to get messed up." ①②

"Hmm," said Amanda, "Maybe I'll go back home so I can use my own paints." Jada thought for a minute. She decided that she loved spending time with her friend more than she loved keeping her paints perfect. ③

"Actually, you can use mine," said Jada. "I'll get you some paper." The girls had a great afternoon painting. As Jada wiped a little green paint out of the yellow paint later, it reminded her of all the fun she had with her friend. ④

Sometimes a character learns a lesson by having to make a hard choice. Each sentence below is about the choice Jada made. Underline evidence in the passage for each statement using the color indicated.

1. Jada was worried that Amanda might mess up her paint box.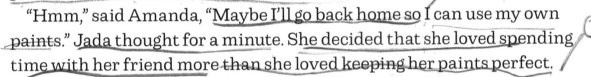

2. Amanda was going to leave if Jada didn't want to share her paints.

3. Jada realizes that friendship is more important to her than having a perfect paint box.

4. Jada's paints did not stay perfect, but that was all right with her.

SKILL: Recount stories, determine the central message

JULIUS AND THE DRAGON: PART I

Once upon a time, there was a village in the mountains. Close by, a dragon named Priscilla lived in a cave. Priscilla spent her time destroying houses with her fiery breath, pulling trees out of the ground, and sending cows flying with a swish of her giant tail. The villagers were tired of Priscilla causing trouble.

One day, Julius, the smallest boy in the village, decided to do something about the dragon. He climbed the hill to the dragon's cave.

"What do you want, pip-squeak?" snarled Priscilla.

"Someone told me that you're getting old and weak, so I wanted to see for myself," said Julius.

Smoke shot out of Priscilla's nostrils. "I am the strongest, fiercest, mightiest dragon in all the land!" Priscilla roared, ready to gobble up Julius for such an insult. Before she ate him, Priscilla would show Julius that there was nothing weak about her.

Continued in Activity 48…

Write the correct trait under the character name.

Julius	Priscilla
small human brave	strong destructive dangerous prideful

brave
human
destructive
prideful
small
strong
dangerous

SKILL: Describe characters in a story and explain how their actions contribute to the sequence of events

JULIUS AND THE DRAGON: PART 2

Continued from Activity 47…

"Prove your might," said Julius. "I bet you can't even push that boulder off the side of the mountain." Priscilla shoved and leaned, but she couldn't budge the boulder.

"My muscles are tired. Give me a different challenge," said Priscilla.

"Okay. Touch a cloud and get back to the ground in five seconds," said Julius. Priscilla flapped her wings and took off.

When she was back on the ground, Julius said, "Eh, that was nine seconds."

"Dragons aren't even meant to fly that high!" complained Priscilla.

"All right," said Julius. "One last try. I bet you can't knock me across the valley with your tail." Priscilla pulled her tail back, but she was already tired and winded. As she clumsily swung it forward, Julius jumped over her tail and watched as Priscilla stumbled over the edge of the cliff. She never bothered the villagers again.

Fill in the empty word shapes below to explain how character traits shaped the story's events.

`Priscilla` is prideful. She wants to prove how

`strong` she is to Julius. She tries so hard to prove herself

that she falls off a `cliff`.

`Julius` is brave. His bravery helps him defeat the dragon

even though he is the `smallest` boy in the village.

SKILL: Describe characters in a story and explain how their actions contribute to the sequence of events

THE CLEANEST PIG

William was not like the other pigs. He hated the mud and would much rather be clean. William lived at Meadowgrove Farm where all the other animals were excited for the upcoming mud wrestling championship.

The thought of rolling around in the mud made William's skin crawl. He didn't want to let down the other pigs, but he couldn't imagine himself mud wrestling.

On the day of the competition, William was called to the mud pit. Grayson, his competitor, was already belly-deep in filth. William took off running the other way. Grayson chased after him and the spectators followed. When Grayson rounded the corner of the barn, there was William with a hose.

The crowd followed and cheered, "Water fight!" No one was disappointed that the mud-wrestling championship turned into a friendly battle with hoses and buckets. Everyone ended up a lot cleaner, too.

This story ends with a water fight because William is not like the other pigs and doesn't like to be dirty. Draw or write how you think the story would end if William was like the other pigs.

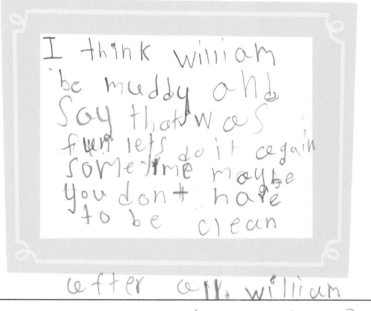

I think william be muddy and say that was fun lets do it again some time maybe you dont have to be clean

after all william learned a lesson.

SKILL: Describe characters in a story and explain how their actions contribute to the sequence of events

GIFTS FROM GRANDMA

Grandma brought an unusual gift for Sienna every time she visited, such as a blinking Christmas light necklace. Another time, Sienna got a squishy penguin toy. Sienna was too old to enjoy most of the gifts, but she appreciated that Grandma thought of bringing her something special. Sienna tossed the gifts in a basket.

One day, Sienna babysat a little boy named Justin. Afterward, she said, "Mom, it's so hard to keep little Justin entertained. He's always getting into things he's not supposed to have."

Her mom said, "When I was a babysitter, I would bring a special bag of toys that the kids had never seen before."

"Good idea!" said Sienna. Sienna brought her whole basket of gifts from Grandma the next time she watched Justin. He squished the penguin, twirled the Christmas light necklace, and stayed out of trouble. The new toys kept him very busy!

Each cause and effect statement below has one word that is wrong. Cross out the mistake and write in the correct word.

1. Sienna ~~didn't~~ *did not* play with the gifts because she was too ~~young~~ *old* for them.

2. Justin got into ~~things~~ *gifts* because it was easy to keep him busy.

3. Sienna brought the special toys because ~~Grandma~~ *mom* suggested it.

4. Bringing the toys caused Justin to be ~~bored~~ *busy*.

SKILL: Describe characters in a story and explain how their actions contribute to the sequence of events

HENRIETTA'S TURN AROUND

Henrietta had a **prickly** personality. She kicked sand, yelled at the frogs, and wouldn't share any of her bug snacks. Other hedgehogs tried inviting her to play games, asking her what was wrong, and even telling her that she looked beautiful. None of it changed Henrietta's behavior. After experiencing so many outbursts and rude interactions, the other hedgehogs began to **detest** Henrietta. They didn't like someone who was so unpleasant.

One day, Henrietta's dad took her to the dentist.

"Oh my!" said the dentist. "Henrietta has a terrible cavity. I bet it's been **distressing** her." Henrietta had the cavity filled. The next day, Henrietta played nicely in the sandbox. She greeted the frogs with a **cordial** wave and a smile. She offered extra bug snacks to another hedgehog who didn't have any. The other hedgehogs were **befuddled**. They couldn't image what had caused such a turnaround in Henrietta, but they liked it!

Draw lines to connect each word to its opposite. If you don't know the meaning of a word, look to see how it was used in the story.

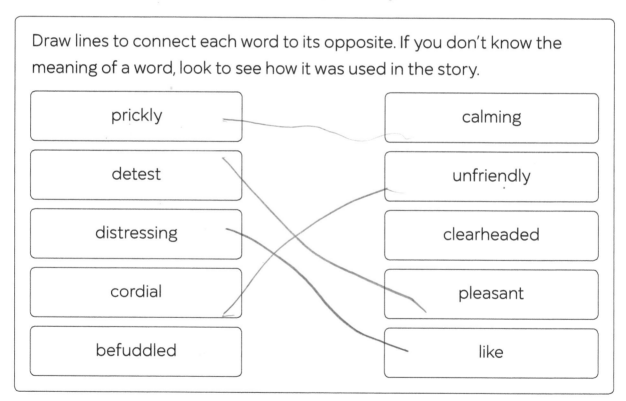

prickly	calming
detest	unfriendly
distressing	clearheaded
cordial	pleasant
befuddled	like

SKILL: Determine the meaning of words and phrases as they are used in a text

THE SPRING CARNIVAL

Every spring, Anthony's mom and some of the other parents from school put together a carnival.

This year, Anthony said, "We need better games at the carnival."

"Maybe you should **coordinate** it then," said his mom. Anthony **seized** the opportunity. He **recruited** other kids in his class. They had meetings at lunch where they planned games, decorations, food, and prizes. Some kids got tired of the **arduous** planning process and quit coming to the meetings. That left more jobs for Anthony. On the day of the carnival, Anthony had to run one of the games himself. His mom walked by his booth.

"I'll be stuck here all night, Mom," **lamented** Anthony.

"It's hard work putting together a carnival, isn't it?" said his mom. "I'll run your game for a while so you can go enjoy yourself," she suggested.

"Thanks, Mom!" said Anthony. "Maybe next year the kids and the grown-ups can work on the carnival together."

Complete the crossword puzzle using the bolded words from the story. You can match the words below with the bolded words from the story to figure out which word goes where.

1. took
2. complained
3. difficult
4. gathered up
5. organize

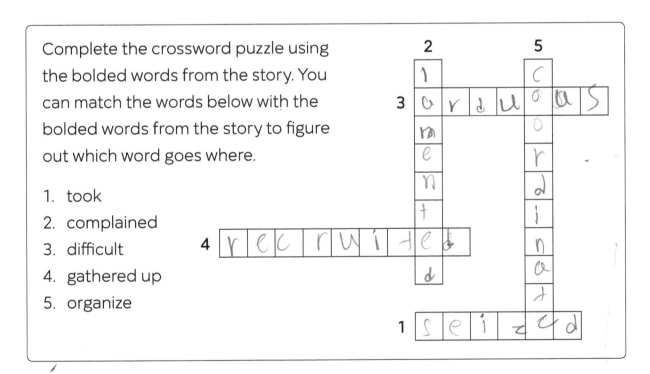

DAVID'S BIG IDEA

There are many sayings that don't mean exactly what the words describe. For each bolded saying, color the check next to the definition that makes the most sense in the story.

David's class was studying ancient Egypt. Everyone had to complete a project at home. David announced, "I'm going to make a pyramid out of cake for my Egypt project!" His mom said, "Do you know how to bake a cake?" His sister said, "**You're biting off more than you can chew**. I think you should come up with a different idea."	☑ David is eating big bites of something. ☑ David is trying to do something that is too difficult.
They really thought David was **off his rocker**, but he believed he could do it. Over the next few weeks, David watched baking shows and made practice cakes. One cake burned, one collapsed, and another was lopsided, but with each try, David learned something.	☑ David is behaving strangely. ☑ Davis is fell off a chair.
David called everyone into the kitchen the night before the project was due. They were surprised to see a pyramid cake, complete with brown-sugar sand. "Well, **color me impressed**!" said David's mom. The next day, David's class admired his creativity. They enjoyed looking at, and eating, his pyramid cake.	☑ David's mom wants to be painted on. ☑ David's mom is amazed.

SKILL: Determine the meaning of words and phrases as they are used in a text

THE WIND'S WAY

Wind is sneaky,
Sifting and stirring but never seen, itself.
It hides in plain sight,
Sighing through screen doors,
Bullying branches into flinging fits.
Don't bother scolding the wind,
By shaking a frustrated finger.
You'll only be pointing,
At its crafty deeds,
While it whips away,
In invisible glee.

This poem describes wind using actions, feelings, and characteristics that only a human could really have. This is called personification. It helps the reader think about wind in a new way. In the word search below, find nine words from the poem that describe wind as if it's a person.

B	Q	H	A	Z	W	S	X	E
U	C	I	S	N	E	A	K	Y
L	R	D	I	D	C	R	F	V
L	A	E	F	T	G	B	Y	H
Y	F	S	T	I	R	I	N	G
I	T	N	I	D	E	E	D	S
N	Y	U	N	G	L	E	E	J
G	S	I	G	H	I	N	G	M

MAKE A METAPHOR

A metaphor is a comparison used by authors to say that one thing is actually something different. For example, "Snow is a white blanket." Draw lines from each metaphor to the item that would best complete it.

Andrew walks down the hall so slowly. He is a _turtle_.

I can't leave the house because I broke my foot. This injury is a _chain_.

Instead of being light and fluffy, the loaf of bread was a _brick_.

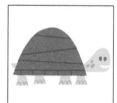

Zahara danced gracefully. She was a _butterfly_ on the stage.

Mateo stood big and strong against the other football players. He was a _mountain_.

SKILL: Determine the meaning of words and phrases as they are used in a text

SUPER FLY: SETTING

The next few activities involve comparing two stories about the same character. One text is in yellow, the other in blue. Read the beginning of both stories and look for details about the setting. Then, draw a picture of each setting in the picture frames below.

Super Fly sat on top of a light post listening to the cars rush by on the street below. This was the perfect place for a bug like him to keep an eye on the city. People were out getting something for lunch. Just then, something caught his eye.

Life was stressful for a crime-fighting insect like Super Fly. He was enjoying some time off in the country—or so he thought. Super Fly was taking a lazy ride around the pasture on the back of a horse when he realized that something smelled unusual . . . and it wasn't the livestock.

Continued in Activity 57 . . .

SKILL: Compare stories written about the same characters

SUPER FLY: PLOT

Continued from Activity 56…

The door of the bank burst open and a man in a mask ran out. He was carrying heavy bags. *A robber!* thought Super Fly. He might be tiny, but he had to find a way to stop the thief.

Super Fly took off to investigate. As he flew closer to the trees, the smell of smoke grew stronger. A fire was burning in the forest! Super Fly couldn't lift a hose or a bucket of water, but he had to find a way to put out the fire.

Mark the passages according to the directions below.

1. Draw an arrow to the characters mentioned in both texts.

2. Underline the character versus nature problem.

3. Draw a star by the character versus character problem.

4. Circle statements about how Super Fly's size impacts the story.

Continued in Activity 58…

SKILL: Compare stories written about the same characters

SUPER FLY: THEME

Continued from Activity 57…

Super Fly couldn't tackle the robber, but he aimed straight for the robber's ear. The robber dropped his bags and scratched frantically at his ear. This gave the police time to arrive and arrest him. Super Fly was a hero!

Super Fly flew inside a nearby market. He nudged a broom, which hit the fire alarm and set it off. Everyone ran outside. Someone noticed the forest fire and called for help. A tiny fly had saved the day!

Arrange the words below into the blanks to describe the theme of both stories.

Word bank:

creative

small

help

important

Even if you are <u>small</u>, you can do <u>important</u> things that <u>help</u> other people if you get <u>creative</u>.

SKILL: Compare stories written about the same characters

NEST-BUILDING ANIMALS

Some people are surprised to learn that birds aren't the only animals that build nests. Animals build nests to protect their babies from the weather and to keep them hidden from predators. Sea turtles dig a hole in the sand to make a nest. After they lay their eggs, they completely cover the nest with sand. The babies have to dig their way back out.

Alligators also make nests by digging a hole. They lay their eggs and cover them in mud and rotting plant material. When the mud dries, it gets hard. Alligator mothers come back and help the babies break through the mud.

Wasps are another nest-building animal. They make their nests out of a papery material. Their nests are complex with individual cells, like a tiny room for each baby. Some wasp nests have many layers of these cells.

Nest-building animals are creative architects who use available materials.

Using the information in the text to write the name of the animal that deserves each award.

Experts at gathering building materials	Nests look the most like a hotel	Strongest diggers as babies
wosp	Sea turtles	Aligator

SKILL: Ask and answer questions to demonstrate understanding of a text, referring explicitly to the text

LADY LIBERTY

The Statue of Liberty is a well-known symbol of the United States. The 151-foot-tall statue was made in France and then taken apart and shipped to the United States in many pieces. The Statue of Liberty was placed on an island in New York Harbor. As people moved to the United States from other countries, many of them passed by the statue in ships. The Statue of Liberty welcomed immigrants to a country of freedom and opportunity.

The Statue of Liberty is not solid. It has a "skin" of copper on the outside and a metal frame on the inside. Over time, exposure to air and water has turned the statue from brown to the green-blue color that we see today. The flame in the statue's torch has been replaced more than once. The current flame is covered in gold and lit at night. The statue represents freedom and is often called Lady Liberty.

If the statement is true, color the check. If the statement is false, color the X.

1. The Statue of Liberty was made in the United States.

2. The Statue of Liberty is located on an island.

3. The Statue of Liberty started out a brown color.

4. The flame in the torch is not the original flame.

SKILL: Ask and answer questions to demonstrate understanding of a text, referring explicitly to the text

HOW HIBERNATION WORKS

All animals take in food and use it to make energy. In the winter, there is less food available for animals. They must do something different in order to survive. Some animals hibernate to survive. Hibernation is different from sleeping. When an animal hibernates, its breathing and heart rate slow and its body temperature drops. All of these changes allow the animal to survive on less energy.

Animals know when to hibernate based on air temperature, the amount of daylight, and their food supply. They make special preparations for hibernation. Some animals, like squirrels, make a den for hibernation. Others dig tunnels, find caves, or go into hollow trees. Some animals store food and briefly wake up during hibernation to eat it. Others eat a large amount of food to store up fat before hibernation. Hibernation is an example of how animals find unique ways to survive in their environment.

Fill in the empty word shapes below to complete the statements about the text.

Hibernating helps animals burn less amount. During

hibernation, an animal's temporture and heart rate

slow down. Air hibernation can help animals

know when to hibernate. Animals who eat a lot before hibernation

are storing up ___.

SKILL: Ask and answer questions to demonstrate understanding of a text, referring explicitly to the text

SEEDS ON THE MOVE

Seeds need their own space to grow. Many seeds have special features that help them move around and spread. Some seeds are shaped like parachutes or wings, so they can float away on the wind. Maple seeds work like this. Some seeds float on water to a new place. Coconuts are seeds that can float to a new place to grow.

People and animals can help move seeds. Seeds that are prickly stick to animal fur or people's clothing. When people or animals walk around, these seeds hitch a ride to a new place. Many seeds, like some berry seeds, are covered in fruit. An animal eats the seed and moves around. The seed comes out in the animal's waste in a new place. Squirrels take acorn seeds and bury them for later. Not all of the acorns are found before they grow into new plants. Seeds have a lot of ways to find a spot to grow.

Mark on the illustration according to the statements below.

1. Draw a star by the seed that travels on wind.

2. Draw arrows to the seeds a small animal could move around.

3. In the blank space, draw a seed that travels on water.

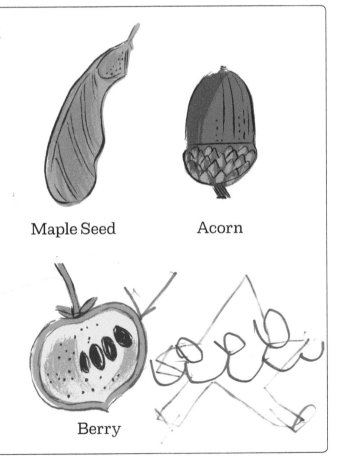

Maple Seed   Acorn

Berry

SKILL: Ask and answer questions to demonstrate understanding of a text, referring explicitly to the text

ALL ABOUT JOINTS

A human adult skeleton has 206 bones. Where two bones meet there is a joint. Joints allow the skeleton to be flexible. There are different kinds of movable joints in the human body. Hinge joints move the way a door opens and closes. Knees and elbows are hinge joints. Pivot joints can rotate or twist. You can turn your head side to side because the bones in your neck have pivot joints. Another kind of joint is the ball-and-socket. In these joints, one bone has a ball shape on the end and the other bone has a hollow space that the ball fits into. Ball-and-socket joints have the widest range of motion. The hip and shoulder are examples of ball-and-socket joints. The thumb is the only place in the body with a saddle joint that rocks back and forth and side to side but doesn't rotate. Joints allow our bodies to move in amazing ways.

Read the passage to someone else. Then, using a pencil tip, hold the loop of a paper clip to the center of the spinner. Flick the paper clip to spin it. Using the question word on the spinner ask a question about the text. See if your listener can answer it.

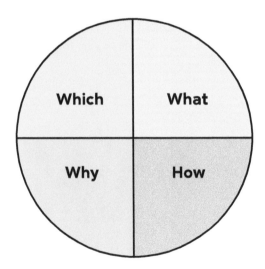

SKILL: Ask and answer questions to demonstrate understanding of a text, referring explicitly to the text

COAST-TO-COAST RAILROADS

Long ago, cars were not yet invented, so people traveled by train or in wagons pulled by animals. There were railroad tracks in both the east and west, but they didn't connect in the center of the country. People decided to complete a transcontinental railroad across the continent. After four years of intense construction, the two tracks met in Utah.

The completion of the transcontinental railroad brought great change to the United States. People and supplies could move much more quickly across the country. The tracks and new settlers also crossed into land that belonged to Native Americans. A more connected country meant new business opportunities for some, but a tragic loss of land and traditional lifestyle for others.

The topic of this passage is the transcontinental railroad. The main idea is what the author wants us to know about the topic. Use the code to complete the main idea.

↑	●	■	▲	◆	♥	⬠	⬡
H	E	T	A	I	N	O	S

Main Idea:

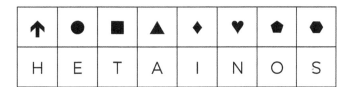

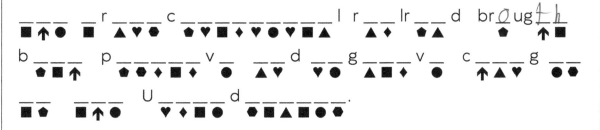

BRIDGES THAT HANG

When a road needs to go across water or a gap in the land, a bridge is built. Engineers can choose from a variety of bridge designs. They use suspension bridges in places where other kinds of bridges wouldn't work.

Suspension bridges have a long deck that hangs from cables. The cables are held up by towers on each end of the bridge. The cables are anchored to the ground as well. One of the biggest advantages of suspension bridges is that they don't need posts or support at the center of the bridge. This means they can span over a body of water and not get in the way of boats. Suspension bridges are also useful for roads over deep canyons where it would be too difficult to build a central support down to the ground. Suspension bridges make road construction possible, even in difficult locations.

Draw the correct symbol in each blank box to complete the statement about the main idea.

=	♥	☺	☾	⚡
distance	bridges	support	span	special

Suspension ☐ are ☐ because they can ☐ across a long ☐ without needing a center ☐ .

SKILL: Determine the main idea and key details

WHY DO WE USE SOAP?

Have you ever tried to shower or bathe with only water? Water alone doesn't get your skin as clean as soap and water together can.

Human skin makes oil and sweat. Skin also comes into contact with dirt and germs. From time to time, it is necessary to get the skin clean. Water is good at washing away dirt, sweat, and some bacteria. However, water doesn't stick to and wash away oil. To test this for yourself, put some cooking oil and some water into a clear container. You will notice that the water and oil stay in separate layers. This is why soap is important.

Soap helps make a connection between water and oil. This allows the water to wash the oil away. Scientists have also found that washing with soap gets rid of more bacteria than washing with water alone. For cleaner skin, make sure to wash with soap!

Create a web between the text's main idea and two supporting details. Circle the yellow main idea that best matches the text. The main idea is what the author wants us to know about the topic. Then, circle two blue details that explain more about the main idea and draw lines to connect them to the main idea circle.

Soap helps water wash away oil.

Showers are better than baths.

You can shower with only water.

Soap smells good.

Soap helps us get our skin clean.

Germs make you sick.

Washing with soap gets rid of more bacteria.

SKILL: Determine the main idea and key details

EARTHWORM WORK

Earthworms may be small and slimy, but they do important work. Earthworms usually stay underground because soil keeps their skin wet. They dig tunnels in soil called burrows. These burrows help water and air get down into the soil. Plants grow better in soil that has plenty of water and air in it.

Earthworms eat the dead parts of plants, like leaves and roots. They break down this dead plant material and release the nutrients back into the soil. These nutrients help new plants grow. Many gardeners purposely add earthworms into their gardens. They put out kitchen scraps like banana peels and apple cores. Earthworms turn this garbage into something called compost, which is rich in nutrients and helps plants grow. Through their diet and everyday activities, earthworms help keep soil healthy. This helps people to grow food.

Mark the following parts of the passage using the colors indicated.

The Topic (just one word)   Green

The Main Idea (a sentence that tells us what the author most wants us to know about the topic)   Blue

A Supporting Detail (tells more about the main idea)   Yellow

Another Supporting Detail (tells more about the main idea)   Red

---

SKILL: Determine the main idea and key details

THE GREAT BARRIER REEF

> ## Location

The Great Barrier Reef is found in the ocean off the coast of Australia. It is over 1,600 miles long. If you could drive along it in a car, it would take a whole day and night to travel its length.

> ## What is a coral?

The Great Barrier Reef is made up of coral. Coral looks like underwater plants, but it is actually tiny animals that make their homes on rocky structures. The animals stay in one place on the reef their entire life. When they die, their bodies add to the reef.

> ## Reef habitat

In addition to the tiny coral animals, the reef is a habitat for other animals and plants. Fish hide from their predators among the coral. Sea grasses grow on the reef. Changing global temperatures and pollution are damaging to the Great Barrier Reef habitat.

Authors use headings to tell what a section will be about. Choose a heading below for each blank box. Some headings will not be used.

What Is Coral?
Jellyfish
Scuba Diving
Reef Habitat
Location

SKILL: Use text features to locate information

COOKBOOK INDEX

bread
    banana 12
    breadsticks 5
    whole wheat 9
chicken
    baked..............14
    fried 3
    soup...............15

lasagna................8
meatballs............2
meat loaf..............4
pork chops............6
stir-fry 10

Notice:

- The index is in alphabetical order
- Subentries show different types of something (like with "bread")

Indexes are found in the back of some books and tell you on what page you will find information on specific topics. Answer each question below by writing in the correct page number. If the math problems are correct, your answers are right!

1. Where would you find how long to cook meat loaf? 4

2. Where would you find the ingredients for meatballs? ✗ 2

3. Where would you find a recipe for lasagna? 8

4. Where would you find a recipe for fried chicken? 3

5. Where would you find out how to make breadsticks? ✗ 5

6. Where would you find out if chicken soup is made with carrots? 15

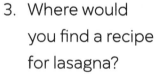

SKILL: Use text features to locate information

HOW LOUD IS TOO LOUD?

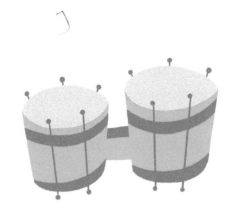

Sound is made when something vibrates. The vibrations move through the air in waves. When the vibrations enter a person's ear, they are perceived as sound. Quiet sounds have small waves and loud sounds have tall waves. Volume measures how loud or quiet a sound is. Volume is measured in units called decibels. The quiet humming of a refrigerator is about 45 decibels. A loud siren is about 120 decibels.

Sounds that are very loud can damage a person's hearing. Hearing can be damaged by exposure to one very loud sound, or by repeated exposure to loud sounds over time. Sounds above 85 decibels are known to cause hearing damage. A lawn mower is about 85 decibels. It's important to wear ear protection like earplugs or noise-reduction earmuffs when you are exposed to loud noises.

Mark the chart according to the instructions below.

1. Draw a horizontal line on the chart to show where 85 decibels would be.
2. Circle the sounds that could cause hearing damage.
3. Draw an arrow to the quietest sound on the chart.
4. Draw a star next to the sounds that are louder than a vacuum.

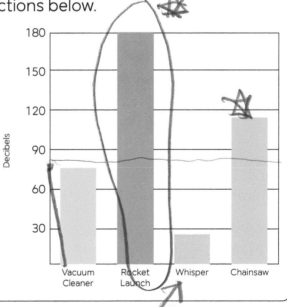

SKILL: Use text features to locate information

WHAT HAPPENED TO THE DINOSAURS?

Destruction from Space

No one knows exactly why all the dinosaurs died or went extinct. One theory is that a huge comet or asteroid struck the Earth. An impact like this would cause extreme heat, fires, and tsunamis. It would create dust and ash clouds that could block out the sun. Dinosaurs would not have survived this kind of destruction.

Volcanoes and Extinction

Some scientists believe that dinosaurs became extinct because of an increase in volcanic eruptions on Earth. Frequent eruptions could push so much gas, ash, and dust into the air that it would block out the sun. Without enough sunlight, plants would die and the temperature would become too cold for dinosaurs.

Use the words from the word bank to complete the comparison of the passages.

Word bank:
ash
~~asteroid~~
~~extinction~~
sun
~~volcanic~~

Both passages are about dinosaur _extinction_. One theory involves the impact of an _asteroid_ while the other is about _____ eruptions. Both passages talk about the ____ being blocked with dust and ____.

SKILL: Compare important points and details in two texts on the same topic

MEASURING MOUNTAINS

Mount Everest

Mount Everest is a popular destination for expert mountain climbers because it is the highest mountain in the world. Mountains can be measured by how much higher they are than the level of the ocean. The point where the ocean meets the land is called sea level. Mount Everest reaches over 29,000 feet above sea level.

Mauna Kea

When volcanoes form on the ocean floor, eventually the lava pushes up and becomes an island. Mauna Kea is a volcanic mountain in Hawaii. It started forming on the ocean floor long ago. If you measure Mauna Kea starting at its base underwater, it is the tallest mountain in the world at about 33,500 feet.

The passages above are both about mountains. Mount Everest is the highest and Mauna Kea is the tallest. Use information from the passages to label the pictures below with the correct mountain name.

Mauna Kea

Mount Everest

SKILL: Compare important points and details in two texts on the same topic

THE CASE FOR AND AGAINST GYM CLASS

Don't Skip this Class

Kids should have gym class at school several times a week. Many kids spend a lot of time on inactive hobbies at home, like playing video games. Gym class gives kids a chance to exercise and learn how to play sports. Without frequent gym classes, kids would be less healthy.

No Time for Gym

Kids spend a limited amount of time at school. Schools need to use as much time as possible for academic subjects like reading, math, and science. When school time is used for gym classes, kids have fewer opportunities to learn important job skills that they will need in the future.

Color the check if the statement is true and the X if the statement is false.

1. Both passages say students should spend more time in gym class.

2. The second passage says gym class teaches job skills.

3. The second passage says gym class time should be spent reading.

4. The two passages state opposite opinions about gym class.

SKILL: Compare important points and details in two texts on the same topic

PONDERING PLASTIC

1. The Perfect Material

Unlike wood or metal, plastic is a material that was invented by people. Plastic is easy to work with because it can be bent and molded into different shapes to make containers, toys, and tools. Plastic doesn't break easily like glass does. It is also lightweight and cheap to make.

2. The Problem with Plastic

When natural materials like wood or cotton are buried in a landfill, they break apart in a few months or years. Plastic takes hundreds of years to break down. Many plastic items, like plastic forks, are meant to be used once. This creates a lot of trash that doesn't break down easily.

Read each statement below and write the passage number(s) that it matches.

1. The topic is plastic. ____

2. The passage shares a negative trait of plastic. ____

3. The passage describes what is unique about plastic. ____

4. The passage shares benefits of plastic. ____

SKILL: Compare important points and details in two texts on the same topic

THE FREE BIKE

Oscar was bored, so his dad told him to go outside and find something to do. He opened his front door and noticed a bike propped up against a streetlight with a sign on it. The sign said, "Free bike! Ride to cure boredom." Oscar had nothing better to do, so he got on.

Oscar had barely put his foot on the pedal when the wheels started spinning out of control and the bike lifted off the ground! Soon, Oscar was high over his neighborhood. He saw new construction going on just down the road. Oscar loved watching the machines. There were kids playing basketball outside of the school. Then, he flew over a sidewalk chalk festival going on at the park. As Oscar flew by the animal shelter, he saw volunteers walking dogs. The bike gently landed on the ground and Oscar climbed off. There was no time to waste. He had a lot to do and see.

Complete the crossword puzzle using the words missing from the sentences below.

1. Oscar's dad sent him _____.
2. The bike he found took him up over his _____.
3. Oscar likes watching construction because of the _____.
4. What were kids playing at the school?
5. At the end, Oscar no longer felt _____ because he realized there was a lot to do and see.

SKILL: Ask and answer questions, referring explicitly to the text

THE DAY I BECAME A TRAPEZE ARTIST

One Saturday at the park, a line of colorful circus trucks pulled up. On each truck, "Donovan Brothers' Circus" was painted in red curly letters.

The ringmaster jumped out and said to me, "Hey kid! I saw the flips you were doing on the bar as we pulled up. Our trapeze artist has the flu. Can you fill in for him?" I looked at my mom and she nodded her head.

"C'mon," said the ringmaster. "We're setting up in the big field over there."

At the circus, I climbed the ladder to the trapeze and realized the net was a lot farther down than the sand at the park! The crowd cheered as I did my flips. Afterward, I found a spot backstage to sit.

"Don't get too comfortable," said the ringmaster, "We've got two more shows to go!" The circus was full of excitement, but I would be glad for a calm day at the park next weekend.

Fill in the empty word shapes below to complete the statements about the text.

This story has two settings: a ⬚⬚⬚⬚ and a ⬚⬚⬚⬚⬚⬚.

The person telling the story is a ⬚⬚⬚ who is good at doing

⬚⬚⬚⬚⬚ on a bar. Working for the circus is hard because

there are ⬚⬚⬚⬚ shows. The kid liked how the circus was

full of ⬚⬚⬚⬚⬚⬚⬚⬚⬚.

SKILL: Ask and answer questions, referring explicitly to the text

NO RUNNING IN THE HALL

One day a cheetah walked into Miller Street School behind some first graders. He found a warm spot by a window and took a nap. Later, the cheetah felt hungry. He got up, stretched, and then sprinted down the hall toward the cafeteria.

"Whoa, whoa, whoa!" said a stern voice. "There is no running in the hall." It was Mrs. Griggs, the principal. The cheetah slowed to a walk and Mrs. Griggs smiled. After recess, when the kids were back in their classrooms, the cheetah heard a knock on the door to the playground. Someone was locked outside! The cheetah hated to break the rules, but he knew he needed to get help. The cheetah found Mrs. Griggs. He circled around her and then ran back down the hall.

Mrs. Griggs followed, shouting, "This is unacceptable!" The cheetah stopped and when Mrs. Griggs caught up she heard the knocking.

She let the student inside and said, "I guess sometimes there's a good reason to break the rules."

Read this story to someone else. Then, ask the listener questions about the text. Color a star for each kind of question you can come up with.

Ask a question about:

☆ characters

☆ setting

☆ conflict or problem

☆ lesson

SKILL: Ask and answer questions, referring explicitly to the text

THOMAS'S TALENT

Thomas looked up to his sister, who was a great artist. He wanted to get a piece of art into an art show just like she had done. Unfortunately, Thomas struggled to get his drawings to look right.

One day, Thomas was outside playing baseball with his friends when his mom called him to leave for his art lesson. "Aw, man!" said his friend. "You're the best hitter we've got."

Thomas's lesson was frustrating. His mom picked him up later and handed him a flyer for baseball league tryouts.

"This would be perfect for you!" she said.

"A baseball league?" asked Thomas. "But how will I get ready for the art show?"

"Maybe you should find your own thing. I would be happy to celebrate you even if it's not at an art show," said his mom.

A couple months later, Thomas slid across home plate, winning the game for his new baseball team. He soaked up the cheers of his teammates and his family, glad to let his own talents shine.

Mark the text above to answer each question using the colors indicated.

1. Why was Thomas so interested in art?   *Blue*

2. What is the problem in the story?   *Yellow*

3. What causes Thomas to consider trying something other than art?   *Red*

4. Why was Thomas happy at the end, even though he was never   *Green*
   featured in an art show?

SKILL: Ask and answer questions, referring explicitly to the text

THE ARMADILLO PRINCE

As a princess leaned over to smell a rose in her garden, her tiara fell off into the thorny branches. An armadillo crawled out from under the rose bush.

"I'll help you get your tiara! The thorns don't scratch my tough shell. In return, I ask that you promise to be my friend," said the armadillo. The princess agreed. After the armadillo retrieved the tiara, the princess took it and skipped back to the castle without another thought of the armadillo.

At dinner, she heard a tapping sound at the door. It was the armadillo, ready to eat with his new friend. The princess was slightly disgusted, but she kept her promise. The next night when the princess answered the door at dinnertime, a prince stood there. He told her that a witch had turned him into an armadillo.

"You broke the curse by befriending me," the prince explained. The princess was glad she had kept her word to the armadillo. She invited the prince to dine with her again and enjoyed having a human dinner guest.

Starting at the arrow, color a path of connected boxes to make a sentence that tells the story's lesson. Stop when you get to a box that touches the stop sign.

→	It	isn't	smart	to	be
never	is	important	if	with	friends
a	when	to	keep	an	armadillo
good	idea	see	your	promises	**STOP**

SKILL: Recount stories, determine the central message

THE MAGIC RING

Nicole got a ring out of a toy vending machine.

  She put it on and said, "I wish I had gotten a yo-yo." Just then, a yo-yo dropped out of the machine. Nicole realized the ring was magic! She stepped outside of the store and two kids zipped past her on scooters.

  "I wish I had a scooter!" said Nicole. A scooter appeared in front of her. As she cruised down the street, she saw a man with a puppy.

  "I wish I had a puppy!" said Nicole. A leash appeared in her hand and the puppy took off running. It was all Nicole could do to keep ahold of the leash and keep her balance on the scooter. The puppy pulled her until she was completely lost. When the puppy finally stopped, Nicole sat down on the curb.

  "I wish everything was back to normal," she said. When she looked up, Nicole found she was in her room. There was no puppy or scooter, but she was much happier.

Sometimes the lesson in a story is shown through what a character learns. Fill in the blanks to complete Nicole's explanation of what she learned.

I learned that instead of _____

_____

_____

_____,

it's better to _____

_____

_____

_____.

SKILL: Recount stories, determine the central message

STONE SOUP: A FOLKTALE

A hungry traveler came upon a village, but found that no one would share any food with him.

"Please bring me a pot of water with a stone in it and I'll make stone soup," said the traveler. The villagers did what he asked. The traveler soon had the pot boiling over a fire.

"This soup would be better with a few potatoes, and it would cook more quickly with some onions," said the traveler. The villagers got a few potatoes and onions and tossed them in.

"It would smell even better with some beef," said the traveler. A man found some beef to add.

"This soup would be fit for a king if it had some carrots," said the traveler. Someone found a few carrots for the soup.

The traveler said, "There's plenty for everyone! Please get bowls and enjoy my stone soup." The villagers all had dinner together and were amazed at how the traveler had turned a stone into soup.

Fill in the blanks to explain what really happened in the text. Use the shapes to find the letters that complete the last sentence.

The villagers were curious about how the _ _ _ _ _ _ _ _ _ _ could make
⬠

soup out of only a _ _ _ _ _ _ and _ _ _ _ _ _ _. The traveler tricked
♥ ● ▲

the _ _ _ _ _ _ _ _ _ _ into adding all the ingredients for _ _ _ _ _
● ■ ◆ ⬆

to the pot.

> The lesson is that _ h _ _ _ _ _ g benefits _ _ _ _ _ y _ _ _ _.
> ⬆ ⬠ ◆ ■ ● ▲ ⬠ ▲ ◆ ♥ ● ▲

MILA AND LUCY'S SLEEPOVER

It was Friday night and Mila's friend Lucy was sleeping over. Mila was worried about her guest getting bored, so she made a list of fun things they could do.

"First on the list is to pop some popcorn!" said Mila. While they were waiting for the popcorn to finish popping in the microwave, Mila accidentally knocked over a glass of water. The water soaked her list and ruined it!

"How will I remember all of my plans now?" complained Mila.

"I'm not worried," said Lucy. "We can think of plenty to do on our own. Why don't we build a blanket fort and eat our popcorn in there?" Mila hadn't even thought of putting blanket-fort building on the list.

Much later, Mila said, "I just remembered, the last activity on the list was watching a movie." The girls agreed that they were so tired from all the other activities they'd thought up that they'd rather just go to sleep.

Add the following marks to the passage above.

☐   Draw a box around the exposition (where the main characters and setting are introduced).

★   Put a star by the climax (the most exciting part of the action).

___   Underline the rising action (where the character runs into a problem).

( )   Put parentheses around the resolution (where the problem is solved).

SKILL: Refer to text organization; describe sequence

CHEERING FOR ANDRE

At every school performance, Andre ran the light board. He made sure the right lights shone at the right time. At the end of each show, Andre felt sad because the crowds clapped and cheered for the performers on stage, but not for him.

One night, Andre decided to stay home instead of going to the spring dance showcase. When the director realized that Andre was missing, he went back to the control room to dim the lights so the show could begin. The director pressed a button and the theater was plunged into total darkness. The audience panicked!

Desperately, the director called Andre and begged him to help. Andre heard the uproar in the background and got to the theater as fast as he could. He dashed into the booth with a flashlight, and in no time, he had the lights dimmed and a spotlight on the stage. The audience cheered for Andre! He sat down as the show started, realizing that it couldn't have happened without him.

Use words or pictures to fill in the blank boxes below.

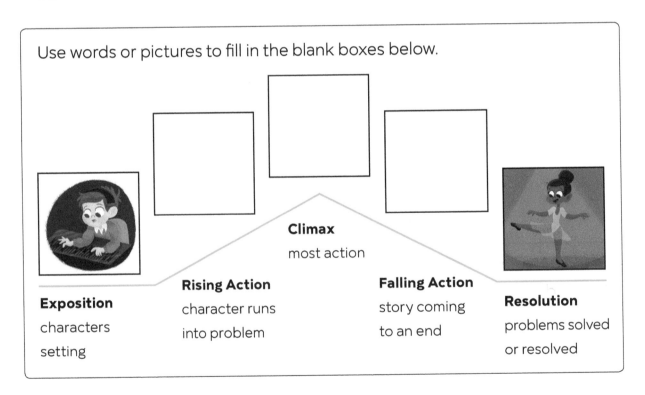

Climax
most action

Rising Action
character runs
into problem

Falling Action
story coming
to an end

Exposition
characters
setting

Resolution
problems solved
or resolved

SKILL: Refer to text organization; describe sequence

BREAKFAST

 Soft sun through the window,
Nudges me awake, reminds me,
It's not a dark school morning,
But Saturday at Grandma and Grandpa's.

 The scent of bacon calls to my stomach,
My hunger tugging me,
From the embrace of the soft bed,
I pad down the blue-carpeted hall.

 A set table and quiet kitchen reveal,
Breakfast has been ready for a while,
But they waited,
Just for me.

★ Looking up from newspapers,
They smile,
And we celebrate a new day,
With fresh melon, pancakes, and cocoa.

A stanza is a set of lines that are grouped together in a poem. Answer each question by drawing the symbol of the correct stanza(s) in the blank.

☐ ☐	☐	☐	☐

These stanzas show how the grandparents treat the poem's narrator:

This stanza shows the setting of the poem:

This stanza shows the reason the narrator got up:

This stanza tells how the narrator knows it's not a normal day:

SKILL: Refer to text organization; describe sequence

IN SEARCH OF A CAMPSITE: ACT I

Characters:
Anna: the mother
Heather: Anna's 10-year-old daughter
Brent: Anna's 7-year-old son

SCENE 1

Setting

A hiking trail, the sun low in the sky. Anna, Heather,
and Brent enter, stage right. All characters are tired from hiking.
Brent: Are we back to the car yet?
Anna: Almost. We covered a lot of miles today!
Heather: I'm looking forward to sitting in my lawn chair at the campsite.
Anna: First we've got to find a campsite.
Anna, Heather, and Brent exit, stage left. — Introduction

SCENE 2

Riding in a car, camping gear piled on top. Sunset. Anna is driving. Heather
and Brent are in the back seat.
Heather: That was the third campground we've driven through, and there's
not a single empty campsite!
Anna: I guess we'll have to keep driving. The map says there's another
campground three miles down the road.
Brent: I'm getting hungry!   *Rising*

Continued in Activity 86 . . .

Color the check if the statement is true and the X if the statement is false.

1. Scene 1 hints at the problem.   ✓ ✗
2. The characters are first introduced in scene 2. ✓ ✗
3. Between scene 1 and scene 2, the setting changes. ✓ ✗
4. The problem gets resolved in scene 2.   ✓ ✗

SKILL: Refer to text organization; describe sequence

IN SEARCH OF A CAMPSITE: ACT 2

Continued from Activity 85...

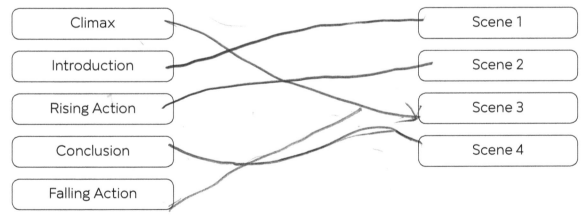

SCENE 3

In the dark, Anna is getting gear off the top of the car.
Anna: Finally! An empty spot.
Heather: How are we going to get the tent up? *Clu*
Brent: I'll hold up a flashlight!
Brent trips on a rock and the light goes out. When it comes back on, Anna and Heather are entangled in the tent.
Anna: I've got a better idea.
Anna goes back to the car and turns it on so that the headlights illuminate the area. Both kids chuckle. — Climax falling

SCENE 4

The tent is now set up. Anna is handing out granola bars. In conclusion
Anna: Sorry, kids, I'm not firing up the cookstove after such a long day.
Brent: Granola bars, chips, and bananas for dinner? I'm not complaining!
Anna and Heather laugh and enjoy their food. — Conclusion

Draw a line to match each plot element with the scene where it is found.
More than one plot element can be found in a scene. Look back to activity 85 if needed.

Climax	Scene 1
Introduction	Scene 2
Rising Action	Scene 3
Conclusion	Scene 4
Falling Action	

SKILL: Refer to text organization; describe sequence

THE KITCHEN TABLE MYSTERY

Below, the same story is told from three different points of view. Read each version and draw a picture of the person telling it.

I followed my son through the door of our apartment after a long day of work.

"Uh, Dad, we have a problem here," said my son. As I turned the corner, I saw that everything that had been on the table was now on the floor! So much for relaxing after work! How did this even happen?

When the humans left for the day, I noticed the smell of peanut butter toast in the kitchen. Dogs can't resist peanut butter, so I tugged the tablecloth to knock the toast off the edge. Suddenly, the mail, books, and empty dishes all fell to the floor. I gobbled the toast and then hid under the bed.

I'm starting to think my apartment is haunted. When I came home with my dad today, it was like a ghost had thrown everything from the table onto the floor. I wonder if this has anything to do with the toast I left on the table this morning.

SKILL: Distinguish their point of view from the narrator's and characters'

THE PARTY AT THE PARK

I cautiously approached the rowdy group of kids crowded around a picnic table. Ellie's mom quieted the group and asked each person to say their name. My heart pounded.

"I'm Clara," I said. I hate talking in front of crowds.

Next, we played a tag game. The sound of kids screaming was hurting my ears. Then, we ran relay races. My team was yelling for me to go faster and it was a lot of pressure. I quietly snuck away to the swings.

"Hey!" said another girl who was sitting on a slide. "I'm Janine. You're one of Ellie's friends, too, right?"

"Yeah," I said. "I just needed a break. I must be the only one that doesn't like noisy games."

"You're not the only one," said Janine. We enjoyed the sunshine and quiet together for a while and then joined the group for cake. Some of the kids started a game of duck-duck-goose while we waited for our parents, but Janine and I sat together at the picnic table and enjoyed talking together.

Read each statement below. If it matches Clara's point of view, circle her name. If it matches your point of view, circle "Me."

1. Talking in front of a group is stressful.   Clara   Me

2. Games with cheering and screaming are fun.   Clara   Me

3. It's boring to spend time with only one other person.   Clara   Me

4. Sitting in quiet is enjoyable.   Clara   Me

SKILL: Distinguish their point of view from the narrator's and characters'

THE DRUM: A FOLKTALE FROM INDIA

Once, a boy asked his mother for a drum, but all she could give him was a magic stick. While walking one day, the boy came across a baker who needed firewood. The generous boy gave his stick to the baker. The baker gave him some bread. Next, the boy came upon a hungry woman. He gave her his bread and in return, she gave him a pot. Then, the boy saw a couple trying to wash clothes with a broken water pot. The boy gave them his pot. In exchange, they gave the boy a coat. Down the road, the boy came across a shivering man without enough clothes. The boy gave the cold man the coat and in exchange, the man gave the boy his horse. Finally, the boy came upon a groom who needed a horse for his wedding march. The boy gave the groom his horse. In return, the groom gave the boy a drum. When he got home, the boy played his mother a song. The boy was wise to give what he had to others.

Find the words that complete each sentence below in the word search.

1. Originally, the boy wanted a _____.
2. Each time he came across a person in need, he _____ them the item he had.
3. When the boy gives away his stick, the narrator describes him as _____.
4. The narrator's point of view is that it was _____ for the boy to give away his things.
5. Do you agree? ___ or __.

Q	A	G	A	V	E	Z	W
S	X	E	D	C	R	F	V
T	G	W	I	S	E	B	Y
Y	H	N	U	D	J	M	E
G	E	N	E	R	O	U	S
I	K	O	L	U	P	O	Q
A	Z	W	S	M	X	E	D
C	R	F	V	T	G	B	Y

SKILL: Distinguish their point of view from the narrator's and characters'

AN UNLIKELY TEAM

In the wild, many mammals work together with their own kind. It is rare to see two different kinds of mammals helping each other. However, warthogs and mongooses are an exception to this rule.

Warthogs are like pigs, but they are wild and have tusks. They live in grassland and savannah habitats. Sometimes tiny bugs called ticks attach themselves to warthogs. Ticks can be painful, bothersome, and carry disease.

Mongooses are long furry animals with pointed faces. They eat insects, along with seeds, nuts, and other small animals. Mongooses help warthogs with their tick problem. Visitors to the Queen Elizabeth National Park in Uganda have witnessed mongooses pulling ticks off warthogs. Warthogs even lay down so that it's easier for the small mongooses to climb on them and find the ticks. The mongoose gets food and the warthog gets rid of bothersome pests. A relationship like this where both animals benefit is called symbiosis.

Complete the crossword puzzle using the clues below.

1. Warthogs have these, but farm pigs don't.
2. Warthogs are bothered by these insects.
3. This is the name for a helpful animal relationship.
4. This is the smaller of the two main animals in the text.
5. What does the mongoose get out of helping the warthog?

SKILL: Ask and answer questions to demonstrate understanding of a text, referring explicitly to the text

A MOUNTAINTOP CITY

High in the mountains of Peru are the ruins of an ancient city called Machu Picchu. Although no one has lived there for hundreds of years, an impressive layout of about 200 stone buildings remain. The structures include palaces, plazas, houses, temples, and even an observatory for studying the sun and stars. Experts believe that Machu Picchu was built as a special home for an Incan emperor and all the people he would have needed to support him.

To make mountaintop living easier, the Inca built large stair steps called terraces around the city. The terraces gave the Inca flat land for growing crops like corn and potatoes. The Inca also guided mountain streams into stone channels and fountains so they would have access to fresh water.

Today, Machu Picchu is a popular destination for tourists. Over one million visitors hike to explore the ruins each year. Experts work to protect the ruins from damage, while still allowing visitors to learn from and enjoy them.

Mark the answer to each question below in the text using the indicated color.

1. Why was Machu Picchu built?   Blue

2. What did the Inca do to make life on a mountaintop possible? (Underline two details.)   Yellow

3. Where is Machu Picchu located?   Green

4. What construction material did the Inca use at Machu Picchu?   Red

SKILL: Ask and answer questions to demonstrate understanding of a text, referring explicitly to the text

CLOWNS OF THE SEA

Good readers look for the answers to things they're wondering about as they read. Before reading the text below, write down a question that the title and picture make you wonder about. If you find the answer to your question as you read, underline it.

My question:

Puffins are unusual-looking birds because they have the black-and-white body of a penguin and a colorful beak like a toucan. They are nicknamed the "clowns of the sea." For most of the year, it's hard to find puffins because they spend their time out in the open ocean. They rest on waves and catch fish to eat.

In the spring, thousands of puffins come ashore in Iceland, an island in the Atlantic Ocean. Puffins dig burrows in the ground instead of building nests. The females each lay a single egg in their burrows. Both the males and females take care of the egg for about 40 days. Then the baby puffins, called pufflings, hatch.

Bird watchers and scientists come to Iceland during the summer to study the birds. Iceland is considered the puffin-watching capital of the world. At the end of the summer, the adult puffins return to the sea and the new puffins eventually follow in search of food.

SKILL: Ask and answer questions to demonstrate understanding of a text, referring explicitly to the text

MAKING MAPLE SYRUP

The delicious golden syrup that you pour on your pancakes comes from inside a tree! Here is how it makes its way to your plate:

All summer, sugar maple trees turn energy from the sun into a kind of sugar. The trees store the sugar in a liquid called sap that runs through their roots and trunks. In early spring, workers drill one or more holes in a sugar maple and push in a spout or a tube in order to capture the sap. The sweet sap comes out of the tree at these drill holes and workers collect it. The sap can be collected at the tree in a bucket or from a series of long tubes that move sap from individual trees into a storage container.

Next, the sap is heated so that much of the water evaporates, leaving sweet syrup behind. Then, the syrup is filtered and packaged in bottles for shipment to grocery stores.

Fill in the blanks to complete each sentence. Use the shapes to find the letters that complete the last fact.

The sticky liquid inside a tree is called __ __ __. It is found in the roots
　　　　　　　　　　　　　　　　　　▲

and __ __ __ __ __ __ __ of trees. Workers drill a hole into the trees so they
　　　　■

can __ __ __ __ __ __ __ the sap. Then, it has to be __ __ __ __ __ __ __ so that
　　　⬟　　　　　　　　　　　　　　　　　　　　　↑

a lot of the __ __ __ __ __ __ evaporates.

Most maple syrup comes from __ __ __ __ __ __ __ __.
　　　　　　　　　　　　　　　　⬟ ▲ ■ ▲ ↑ ▲

TAKING TO THE SKIES

For more than 2,000 years, people have been interested in achieving flight. One of the first examples of man-made flight was kite flying in ancient China. Some kites were even designed to lift people, but they were dangerous. The next advancement in flight involved balloons. Both hydrogen balloons and hot-air balloons could carry people in the air for extended amounts of time.

Later, people experimented with gliders, which were unpowered aircraft. Gliders had to be launched from a hill or a balloon and could glide for a short distance in the air. Soon, humans achieved powered flight. Orville and Wilbur Wright designed airplanes with an engine-powered propeller. They also developed ways to control the direction of the flight. During World War II, airplanes were upgraded with jet engines. Jet engines allowed planes to fly farther and faster than before. More recently, computers have been used for controlling planes both on board and from the ground. Over time, humans have made incredible progress in flight.

Draw a line from each clue to the matching picture.

Airplane feature before World War II

Flight method before gliders

Earliest man-made flight

After airplanes with propellers

SKILL: Describe sequential and cause and effect relationships in text

HOW THE TEDDY GOT ITS NAME

The teddy bear gets its name from the 26th United States president, Theodore Roosevelt. In 1902, President Roosevelt went on a hunting trip in Mississippi with a group of his friends. The group didn't see any animals for most of the trip. Finally, some of the people in the group surrounded and tied up a black bear. They invited President Roosevelt to shoot the bear. Roosevelt loved the outdoors and did not think it was fair to hunt an animal who was tied up, so he refused to shoot the bear.

The story of Roosevelt and the bear spread across the country, even becoming the topic of a newspaper cartoon. When a store owner in New York heard the story, he decided to make toy bears to sell in his shop. After asking permission from President Roosevelt, the store owner named the toys "teddy" bears since Teddy is short for Theodore. Teddy bears are still popular toys today.

Fill in the word shapes to complete the cause and effect relationship.

Cause

President

☐☐☐☐☐☐☐☐

went on a ☐☐☐☐☐☐

trip with friends but chose not to

shoot a tied up ☐☐☐☐.

Effect

A store owner made ☐☐☐

bears in his honor and called

them ☐☐☐☐ bears.

SKILL: Describe sequential and cause and effect relationships in text

WHY DO WE SWEAT?

On a hot day or after exercising, you may notice that your skin is a little bit wet. This is sweat, and although it seems gross, it's actually very useful! The human body works best at 98.6 degrees Fahrenheit. When the brain notices that the body is heating up, it takes action to cool it back down.

First, the brain tells the sweat glands to release sweat. Sweat travels to the surface of the skin through tiny openings called pores. After sweat reaches the surface of the skin, it evaporates into the air. When the sweat evaporates, it takes some body heat with it, causing the body to cool down. This is why fanning yourself helps you stay cool. The fan moves more air past your skin, helping the sweat evaporate and removing body heat.

Sweat is made of mostly water. It is important to drink extra water to replace what was lost through sweating. Sweat is your body's way of keeping you from overheating without you even having to think about it!

Each sequence statement below has one word that is wrong. Cross out the mistake and write in the correct word.

1. Before sweat gets to the surface of the skin, it evaporates.

2. Lastly, the brain tells the sweat glands to make sweat.

3. After the body can cool down, the pores have to release sweat.

4. First, the sweat evaporates and removes some body heat.

SKILL: Describe sequential and cause and effect relationships in text

PREDICTING THE WEATHER

Weather reports help people know what to wear and what kind of activities to plan. Scientists called meteorologists look for patterns in order to predict the weather. They use air temperature to make predictions. When a warm body of air meets a cold body of air, a storm is likely.

Meteorologists also use atmospheric pressure to predict weather. Atmospheric pressure measures how much the tiny molecules in the atmosphere are pressing down on an area of the planet. If the air pressure rises, the weather will probably be calm with clear skies. When the pressure drops, there is a good chance of storms.

The condition of the sky can also be used to predict weather. If clouds are getting thicker, rain is likely in the near future. When there is fog in the morning, the weather will usually be fair later in the day. If a rain storm is coming in, the fog will be blown away by pre-storm winds. Patterns in temperature, pressure, and cloud cover help meteorologists predict the weather.

Complete the cause and effect relationships by adding words or pictures in the blank boxes below.

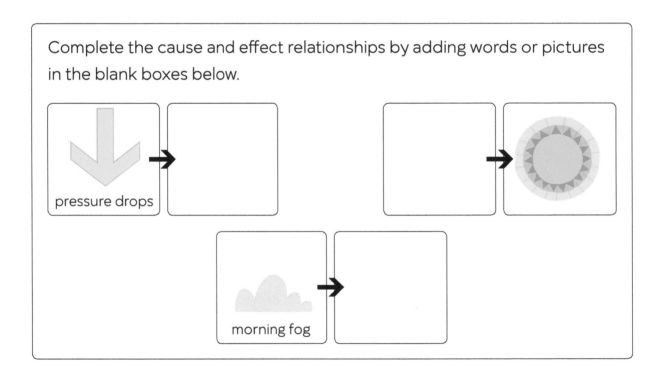

pressure drops

morning fog

SKILL: Describe sequential and cause and effect relationships in text

SALT DOUGH SCULPTURES

Salt dough is fun to sculpt and build with. You can make it at home.

Ingredients:
1 cup salt
2 cups flour
¾ cup water

Instructions:
1. Preheat the oven to 325°F.
2. Mix the salt and flour together in a large bowl.
3. Add the water.
4. Stir the mixture until it has a doughy texture.
5. Sculpt something out of the dough.
6. Bake your creation in the oven for an hour. (Ask an adult for help.)
7. Paint your sculpture after it cools.

Draw lines to connect sets of three squares: a picture, a sequence word, and then another picture to match the steps in the text. Lines can be vertical, horizontal, or diagonal. There are four sets of three squares to connect.

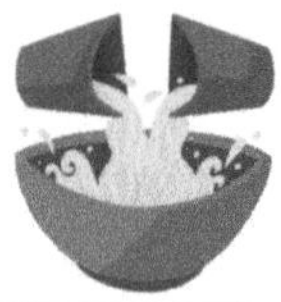	before	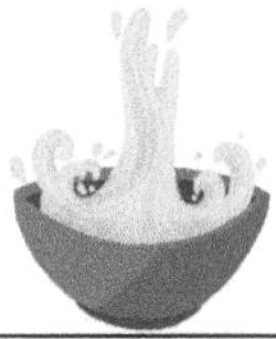	
after	then		after
	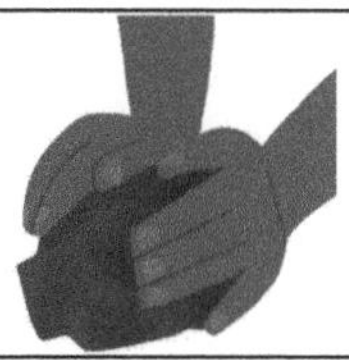	then	

SKILL: Describe sequential and cause and effect relationships in text

FROM COTTON FIELDS TO FABRIC

Cotton, the material that makes up much of your clothing, is grown on farms. Cotton plants grow and flower. When the flowers fall off the plants, a pod called a **cotton boll** is left behind. After a couple of months, the bolls break open. Inside the boll is the cotton fiber. Machines harvest the cotton fibers off the plant. Next, the cotton is dried and cleaned.

At a **textile mill**, the cotton is spun into yarn and then woven or knitted into cloth. At this point the cloth is a plain off-white color. Fabrics get their color or print from **dye**. If the cloth is meant to be one color, it is submerged in the dye and takes on the intended color. Fabrics with a print are sent through a machine that is like a paper printer. The machine uses dye to print the pattern on long rolls of fabric. The fabric can then be cut and sewn to make clothing and other products.

Label each picture below with the correct bolded word from the text.

SKILL: Determine the meaning of domain-specific words and phrases

A CLOSE LOOK AT MUSHROOMS

Mushrooms look like plants, but are actually a type of organism called a fungus. Fungi are different from plants because they don't make food from sunlight. Instead, fungi absorb their food from dead plants.

There are many kinds of mushrooms, but gilled mushrooms are the most familiar. Underground, gilled mushrooms have threadlike parts called mycelia that absorb food. When the temperature, humidity, and nutrient level are right, the mycelium sends up a fruiting body that we call a mushroom.

Gilled mushrooms are held up by a stem. On top of the stem is a cap. If you look closely under the cap you can see thin lines called gills. Mushrooms make seeds called spores. The spores are formed in the gills of a mushroom. When the spores are released from the gills, they can float away on the wind. If the spores land in a place with dead plant material and moisture, they can form new mycelium underground and grow more mushrooms.

Mark the diagram above according to the statements below.

1. Circle the part that can grow into new mushrooms.

2. Draw an arrow to where the spores are made.

3. Draw a box around the part that absorbs food.

4. Draw a star by the part that holds the mushroom up.

SKILL: Determine the meaning of domain-specific words and phrases

POWER FOR THE FUTURE

Humans use energy to light houses, power factories, fuel cars, and for many other purposes. Energy comes from either renewable or nonrenewable resources. Renewable resources will never run out. For example, people can make energy from wind and the sun. Wind turbines use the movement of the wind to make electricity. Solar panels collect energy from the sun. These resources don't run out.

In contrast, nonrenewable resources will run out someday. Fossil fuels are nonrenewable. Fossil fuels are made of plant and animal matter that was buried under the Earth a long time ago. Heat and pressure changes underground turned this matter into coal, oil, and natural gas. Humans dig and pump fossil fuels out of the ground and then burn them to make energy. For example, gasoline is made from the fossil fuel oil. Someday there won't be any fossil fuels left underground. It is important for people to move toward developing and using more renewable resources before fossil fuels run out.

Color the check if the statement is true and the X if the statement is false.

1. Fossil fuels will never run out.

2. Solar panels collect wind energy.

3. Renewable resources can be used again and again.

4. Turbines are used to collect a renewable energy source.

SKILL: Determine the meaning of domain-specific words and phrases

ICE AGE GIANTS

Long ago, the Earth went through a period of colder temperatures. Much of the water on Earth froze into **glaciers**. A set of large animals called **megafauna** lived on the Earth at this time.

One example is the giant beaver, which looked like a modern-day beaver except that it was the size of a bear. Woolly mammoths were similar to modern elephants, but they were covered in fur so they could survive in cold temperatures. There were also woolly rhinoceroses during the Ice Age. The **Smilodon** was about the size of a modern-day tiger. It had especially long **canine teeth**. Many of the big mammals from the Ice Age are now extinct.

Glossary

canine teeth – pointed teeth near the front of the mouth

glacier – a giant mass of ice

megafauna – animals that weigh at least 97 pounds

Smilodon – also known at the saber-toothed tiger

Underline the glossary word that matches each clue below in the indicated color.

1. The Smilodon had especially long ones   *Blue*

2. The giant beaver was part of this group   *Yellow*

3. This was caused by cold temperatures on Earth   *Red*

4. An animal the size of a tiger   *Green*

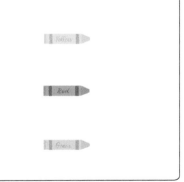

SKILL: Determine the meaning of domain-specific words and phrases

WHY ZOOS MATTER

A fact is something that is true and can be proven. For example: Birds have wings. An opinion is how someone feels about something. Other people might feel differently. For example: Birds make the best pets. For each statement below, color *F* if it is a fact and *O* if it is an opinion.

Zoos are not the natural habitat of wild animals.	F O
However, zoos are beneficial for both humans and animals.	F O
Zoos bring people into close contact with wild animals that they might not see otherwise.	F O
People might not understand how important it is to protect animals if they never see how amazing the animals are.	F O
Zoos provide a place for scientists to study animals.	F O
With better information, scientists can help support other animals that are in the wild.	F O

SKILL: Distinguish own point of view from that of the author

HOMEWORK PROBLEMS

When the final school bell rings, kids should be done with school for the day. However, it is common to see kids at home working on books, papers, and computers to complete their homework. After kids have worked hard at school all day, their brains are tired and they should have a break.

Kids need time to do things that they can't do at school, such as helping and playing with family members and participating in sports. If kids are too busy with their homework in the evenings, they don't have time for these beneficial activities.

Finally, homework leads to unnecessary stress for kids. Parents and kids argue about when and how to do homework. Keeping up with homework as well as grades can cause anxiety. Homework should be eliminated so that kids can have a healthy balance of academic and nonacademic activities in their lives.

Find the words that complete each sentence in the word search below.

1. The author's opinion is that homework should be _____.
2. After school, kids' brains are _____.
3. Kids need time to help their _____ members.
4. The author says homework leads to _____.
5. How do you feel about the author's opinion? (Circle "agree" or "disagree" in the word search.)

Q	T	I	R	E	D	A
Z	W	D	S	L	X	E
S	D	I	C	I	R	F
T	V	S	T	M	G	B
R	F	A	M	I	L	Y
E	Y	G	H	N	N	A
S	U	R	J	A	M	G
S	I	E	K	T	O	R
L	P	E	Q	E	A	E
Z	W	S	X	D	C	E

SKILL: Distinguish own point of view from that of the author

KIDS AND SCREEN TIME

Televisions, smartphones, tablets, and other computers are part of everyday life. It's important that kids have only one hour of screen time each day. Screen time might negatively impact children's health. Kids may eat absentmindedly during screen time instead of eating to satisfy their hunger. Also, advertisements that appear during screen time can persuade kids to eat food that is unhealthy. Kids are less physically active when they are using a digital device, which can lead to poor health. It's important for kids to spend time using both their large and small muscles for proper development.

Screen time also might cause children to get less sleep. If children are using electronic devices at bedtime, they may be too stimulated to fall asleep. Children may want to keep watching videos or playing games instead of sleeping. To keep kids healthy, parents should only allow them to have one hour of screen time a day.

Draw lines to connect the boxes that explain how you feel about the author's message.

| I agree |
| I disagree |
| I partly agree |

| with the author. |

| I think screen time |

| is |
| is not |
| should be somewhat limited. |

| safe. |
| dangerous. |

SKILL: Distinguish own point of view from that of the author

PLASTIC BAG BAN

Determine if each section below describes something unique to plastic bags, something unique to reusable bags, or something the two have in common. Then, color the corresponding part of the Venn diagram (P is for plastic and R is for reusable).

Most stores offer both plastic bags and reusable bags.	P ⬭⬭ R
Plastic bags are used once and then take up space in a landfill.	P ⬭⬭ R
In contrast, reusable bags can be used again and again without creating a lot of trash.	P ⬭⬭ R
Reusable bags cost more money, but it's worth it in order to reduce waste.	P ⬭⬭ R
Both kinds of bags will help get groceries into your house.	P ⬭⬭ R
Stores should ban plastic bags that get tossed after one use.	P ⬭⬭ R

SKILL: Describe the logical connection between parts of a text

TOO MUCH TESTING

Toward the end of every school year, students participate in many hours of testing to see what they have learned during the school year. The large amount of testing causes problems for students rather than helping schools improve.

There is so much pressure to get high scores on math and reading tests that schools tend to take time away from other important subjects, like social studies and the arts. Also, teachers feel pressured to spend a lot of time teaching test-taking skills rather than skills that will help kids in real life. Some kids have anxiety about taking tests, so their scores do not really show their abilities.

Standardized testing materials have to be purchased and graded, which costs states a lot of money. This leaves states with less money for books, supplies, and teachers. The amount of testing that students go through each year should be greatly reduced to improve their education.

Complete the crossword puzzle with the missing words from the sentences below.

1. Because tests focus on math and reading, less time is spent on social studies and the ____.
2. Pressure causes teachers to spend a lot of time teaching ____ _____ skills.
3. If a student has _____ about testing, their scores may not show their abilities.
4. The purchase of testing materials leaves less _____ for other things schools need.

COMPUTERS IN THE CLASSROOM

Imagine only getting information from the books you had on hand. This is what classrooms were like before the introduction of computers. Computers have become the most important development in education.

Computers first appeared in classrooms in the 1980s, took up a lot of space, and ran simple learning games. About 10 years later, the Internet caught on and many school computers connected to it. Students and teachers accessed information from websites across the world. In the Internet's early days, most of the available information was text, and sometimes images.

As technology improved, computers got smaller and faster. Laptop and tablet computers became available. Students can now stream videos, send messages, and access information from across the globe on a device that is smaller than a book. Online classrooms mean that students don't even need to be in the same location as their teacher. Information and learning opportunities have never been more accessible.

Each sequence statement below has one word that is wrong. Cross out the mistake and write in the correct word.

1. The earliest classroom computers were small.

2. Ten years after computers appeared in schools, many schools got encyclopedia access.

3. Eventually, classroom computers got smaller and slower.

4. Today, students can get information from across the state right in their classroom.

SKILL: Describe the logical connection between parts of a text

DESIGNING SMARTER CITIES

Many cities are designed with big neighborhoods that are far away from where people work and shop. This means that people have to make frequent long car trips in order to meet their needs. Pollution from all of these car trips makes our air dirty.

People need communities that are designed for mixed use. This means that places to live are mixed in with places to work and play. One solution is to have tall buildings with stores and other workplaces on the street level and housing on the upper levels. Another way to make mixed-use communities is to have several smaller stores that can be supported by the people living nearby rather than big stores that have to draw people in cars from far away.

The best way to reduce pollution from cars is to design communities where people can walk or take short car trips to get to the places they need to go.

In the text above, the first paragraph presents a problem and the second paragraph gives a solution. In the space below, draw what a neighborhood might look like if it was designed to match the solution presented in the text.

SKILL: Describe the logical connection between parts of a text

LOOK FOR THE RELATIONSHIP

Draw lines to connect each pair of sentences with the picture showing their relationship.

It's expensive for schools to maintain and operate their own fleet of school buses. A less expensive option is to provide students with passes to ride city buses.

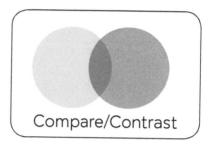

Compare/Contrast

Many restaurants offer water and soda. Both will quench your thirst, but soda has a lot of added sugar.

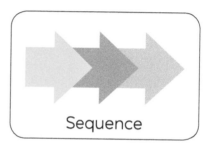

Sequence

The first step toward a better playground is to replace the dirt with woodchips. After that, a new slide needs to be installed.

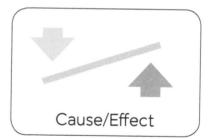

Cause/Effect

Not everyone can use the Internet to help them with homework assignments. Because Internet access is expensive, some kids cannot get online at home.

Problem/Solution

SKILL: Describe the logical connection between parts of a text

Answer Key

1: Lost and Found

1. sunglasses
2. sneaky
3. Isaac
4. watch
5. blocks

2: What Red Said

What was the problem in the story? – Add "Arf" and "Meow" to the speech bubble.

How was the problem solved? – Draw birds at the park around the birdcage.

3: A Shared Lunch

1. "thermos" (yellow)
2. "Alvaro was so hungry" (blue)
3. "grapes", "turkey sandwich" (green)
4. "Alvaro's mom" (red)

4: A Racket on the Tennis Court

Some possible questions and answers:

When did the story happen? – On a summer day

Where did the story happen? – At the park, on a tennis court

Why were the dogs running? – They got away from the boy who was walking them

Where were the dogs running? – To the tennis court and then away from it

When did the dogs give back the balls? – After watching Monica put the ball in the bucket

Why did the dogs give back the balls? – They copied Monica when she put a ball in the bucket

5: After the Rain

Possible questions:

Who donated books to the library?

What did the sign in front of the library say?

Why did everything in the library need to be replaced?

How did the library get new rugs?

6: The Bossy Rooster: A Cuban Folktale

Box 2 – Draw the rooster getting his beak dirty.

Box 3 – Write "No!" in the speech bubble.

Box 4 – Write "Eat the grass!" in the speech bubble.

Box 5 – Draw a stick.

Box 6 – Write "Burn the stick!" in the speech bubble.

7: Frog's Escape

flies, snake, pond, dragonflies

The lesson: When your plans are ruined, something good can still happen.

8: Curtis's Cupcake

Circle these words to find the story's lesson: "Help people even if they make you angry."

9: Waking Up Walter

Somebody – Ned the bear

Wanted – fishing poles

But – Walter is sleeping

So – honey cake

Then – bears eating cake

10: High-Flying Ida

Ida, smaller, balloons, strings, worry

11: Perry's Surprise Disguise

The picture should show a tall boy with brown hair, a tall hat, and a black suit.

12: Evelyn's Answer

Arrows drawn on the dials should show that Evelyn is outdoorsy, active, and loud.

13: Penguin Plunge

1. false
2. true
3. true
4. false

14: Injury and Inspiration

Angel didn't listen to Elias. – Angel didn't learn how to turn on the skateboard.

Angel got X-rays at the hospital. – Angel became interested in being an X-ray technician.

Angel hurt his leg. – Angel had to go to the hospital.

15: Yikes! Spiders!

Bravery Around Spiders – Bryce

Best at Comforting
Others – Mom

Most Dramatic Reactions – Lee

16: A New Home for Alvin

creepy, dreary, cold, empty, damp,
dark, sad

17: Help in the Storm

1. Draw an arrow to the wagon or
   the pioneer clothing.
2. Draw a star next to the
   clear sky or the smile on
   Claire's face.
3. Draw a box around part of the
   open land.
4. Draw a circle around the pot
   over the fire.

18: Spring Break Plans

1. plane
2. dog
3. house
4. feast
5. imagination

19: Kelton's Experiment

1. surprised or shocked
2. messy or dirty
3. Kelton
4. wash the dishes or clean the
   kitchen or clean the mess

20: Walking on the Moon

1. rocket – control module
2. their boots – a flag, a sign,
   or footprints
3. six – three
4. hours – days

21: How the Hippo Got Its Name

"spend most of the day in water"
(yellow)

"long heads with ears, eyes,
and nostrils near the top," "eat
grass" (green)

"long legs and lean bodies," "run
much faster" (blue)

22: Celebrating Holi

colors, India, bonfires, powder

Last sentence: In ancient India,
anyone could throw powder at
the emperor during Holi.

23: Rock Art

Possible questions and answers:

How were petroglyphs made? –
Picking, cutting, or scratching on
rocks with stone tools

What are petroglyphs? – Marks
made by scratching on rocks

Why were petroglyphs made? –
To record stories, make maps, or
record the movement of stars

What can we learn from
petroglyphs? – How prehistoric
people lived

24: From Seed to Christmas Tree

1. false
2. true
3. false
4. false

25: The Lives of Camels

diamond – Camels and People

arrow – Thriving in the Desert

star – Diet

26: Taking a Camping Trip

Encountering Wildlife (yellow)

Recipes (blue)

Outdoor Clothing (green)

Making Shelter (red)

27: Rescuing Baby Elephants

bottles, soccer ball, mud, three
years, wildlife

28: The Rise of the Roller Coaster

1. corkscrew
2. staple
3. suspended
4. imitated

29: Becoming a Butterfly

Label from the top, moving
clockwise: egg, larva, pupa, adult

30: How to Draw a Bird

Pictures will vary

31: A Museum Trip

There are several possible
solutions. All solutions should
include a path through four
exhibits including the dinosaurs,
but excluding the mummies, and
through the café.

32: Animal Long Jumpers

1. impala
2. kangaroo
3. kangaroo
4. human

33: Chuck What?

leaves, fruit, rocks, sand, flowers,
heat, cactus

34: Working as a Veterinarian

Answers will vary

35: Rocks: From Solid to Liquid

The "Before Reading" answers will vary

The "After Reading" answers may include:

Rocks – rocks buried in the Earth melt, can be made of cooled magma

Magma – magma is liquid rock, it cools and forms solid rock, there is a layer of it in the Earth

36: Why We Sleep

Answers will vary

37: From Old Paper to New

Answers or pictures will vary

38: Oh, Deer!

Predictions will vary

39: A Good Start

Kristin feels nervous.

The boy is missing something.

The boy feels sad.

40: The True Story of Cinderella

1. chores
2. stepsister
3. stole
4. return

41: Taking Care of Alyssa

1. false
2. true
3. false
4. false

42: Hurry Up, Henry!

Possible questions:

Who came looking for Henry?

What kind of animal was Henry?

Why was Mother Gorilla always saying "Hurry up, Henry"?

How did Henry find out what he really was?

43: The Clever Beetle

Circle the following:

Somebody – the beetle

Wanted – two beetles

But – the bird

So – "My friend is a snake."

Then – two beetles

44: Theseus and the Minotaur: A Myth

Symbol order: heart, square, circle, arrow, triangle

45: Paul's Report

report, brave, wobbly, stone, thinking

Last sentence: Paul learned that you can be both afraid and brave at the same time.

46: Jada's Paint Box

1. "These are my special paints. I don't want them to get messed up." (yellow)
2. "Maybe I'll go back home so I can use my own paints." (blue)
3. "She decided that she loved spending time with her friend more than she loved keeping her paints perfect." (green)
4. "As Jada wiped a little green paint out of the yellow paint later, it reminded her of all the fun she had with her friend." (red)

47: Julius and the Dragon: Part 1

Julius – brave, human, small

Priscilla – destructive, prideful, strong, dangerous

48: Julius and the Dragon: Part 2

Priscilla, mighty, cliff, Julius, smallest

49: The Cleanest Pig

Answers or pictures will vary

50: Gifts from Grandma

1. young – old
2. easy – hard
3. Grandma – Mom
4. bored – busy

51: Henrietta's Turn Around

prickly – pleasant

detest – like

distressing – calming

cordial – unfriendly

befuddled - clearheaded

52: The Spring Carnival

1. seized
2. lamented
3. arduous
4. recruited
5. coordinate

53: David's Big Idea

David is trying to do something that is too difficult.

David is behaving strangely.

David's mom is amazed.

54: The Wind's Way

sneaky, sifting, stirring, hides, sighing, bullying, crafty, deeds, glee

55: Make a Metaphor

1. turtle
2. chain
3. brick
4. butterfly
5. mountain

56: Super Fly: Setting

Picture 1 – Super Fly should be on a light post with a city street and people below

Picture 2 – Super Fly should be on the back of a horse in a pasture

57: Super Fly: Plot

1. Draw an arrow to "Super Fly" and "robber"
2. Underline "A fire was burning in the forest."
3. Draw a star by "A robber!"
4. Circle "He might be tiny" in the first passage and "Super Fly couldn't lift a hose or a bucket of water" in the second passage.

58: Super Fly: Theme

Even if you are small, you can do important things that help other people if you get creative.

59: Nest-Building Animals

alligators

wasps

sea turtles

60: Lady Liberty

1. false
2. true
3. true
4. true

61: How Hibernation Works

energy, breathing, temperature, fat

62: Seeds on the Move

Draw a star by the maple seed.

Draw an arrow to the berry and the acorn.

Draw a coconut in the blank space.

63: All About Joints

Possible questions:

Which kind of joint is in the thumb?

What can a pivot joint do?

Why do people have joints?

How does a hinge joint move?

64: Coast-to-Coast Railroads

The transcontinental railroad brought both positive and negative changes to the United States.

65: Bridges That Hang

heart, lightning, moon, equal sign, happy face

66: Why Do We Use Soap?

Main idea – Soap helps us get our skin clean.

Details –

Soap helps water wash away oil.

Washing with soap gets rid of more bacteria.

67: Earthworm Work

The Topic – "Earthworms" (green)

The Main Idea – "Through their diet and everyday activities, earthworms help keep soil healthy." (blue)

A Supporting Detail – "They dig tunnels in soil called burrows. These burrows help water and air get down into the soil." (yellow)

Another Supporting Detail – "They break down this dead plant material and release the nutrients back into the soil. These nutrients help new plants to grow." (red)

68: The Great Barrier Reef

Location, What Is Coral, Reef Habitat

69: Cookbook Index

$4 \times 2 = 8$

$3 \times 5 = 15$

70: How Loud Is Too Loud?

Draw a horizontal line a little below the line for 90 decibels.

Circle "rocket launch" and "chain saw."

Draw an arrow to "whisper."

Draw a star next to "chain saw" and "rocket launch."

71: What Happened to the Dinosaurs?

Both passages are about dinosaur extinction. One theory involves an impact with an asteroid while the other is about volcanic eruptions. Both passages talk about the sun being blocked with dust and ash.

72: Measuring Mountains

Label the picture on the left "Mauna Kea" and the arrow 33,500 feet.

Label the picture on the right "Mount Everest" and the arrow 29,000 feet.

73: The Case For and Against Gym Class

1. false

2. false
3. true
4. true

74: Pondering Plastic

1. 1, 2
2. 2
3. 1, 2
4. 1

75: The Free Bike

1. outside
2. neighborhood
3. machines
4. basketball
5. bored

76: The Day I Became a Trapeze Artist

park, circus, kid, flips, three, excitement

77: No Running in the Hall

Possible questions:

Who was the main character in this story?

Where did the story take place?

What problem did the cheetah have?

What lesson did Mrs. Griggs learn?

78: Thomas's Talent

1. "Thomas looked up to his sister who was a great artist." (blue)
2. "Thomas struggled to get his drawings to look right." (yellow)
3. "His mom picked him up later and handed him a flyer for baseball league tryouts." (green)
4. "He soaked up the cheers of his teammates and his family, glad to let his own talents shine." (red)

79: The Armadillo Prince

The lesson: It is important to keep your promises.

80: The Magic Ring

I learned that instead of wishing for things you don't have, it's better to be happy with what you do have.

81: Stone Soup: A Folktale

traveler, stone, water, villagers, soup

The lesson: The lesson is that sharing benefits everyone.

82: Mila and Lucy's Sleepover

Draw a box around the first sentence.

Put a star by the part where Mila spills water on the list.

Underline the sentence that talks about Mila making a list of activities.

Put parentheses around the part where Lucy suggests the girls can come up with activities without the list.

83: Cheering for Andre

Rising Action – Andre stays home

Climax – The director accidentally turns off all the lights and Andre turns them back on

Falling Action – The crowd cheers for Andre.

84: Breakfast

1. square, star
2. triangle
3. circle
4. triangle

85: In Search of a Campsite– Act 1

1. true
2. false
3. true
4. false

86: In Search of a Campsite– Act 2

Climax – scene 3

Introduction – scene 1

Rising Action – scene 2

Conclusion – scene 4

Falling Action – scene 4

87: The Kitchen Table Mystery

Picture 1 – the dad

Picture 2 – the dog

Picture 3 – the son

88: The Party at the Park

Statements 1 and 4 match Clara's point of view. Personal point of view will vary from reader to reader.

89: The Drum: A Folktale from India

1. drum
2. gave
3. generous
4. wise
5. yes or no depending on the reader's opinion

90: An Unlikely Team

1. tusks
2. ticks
3. symbiosis
4. mongoose
5. food

91: A Mountaintop City

1. "Experts believe that Machu Picchu was built as a special home for an Incan emperor" (blue)
2. "the Inca built large stair steps called terraces" and "The Inca also guided mountain streams into stone channels and fountains" (yellow)
3. "High in the mountains of Peru" (green)
4. "stone" (red)

92: Clowns of the Sea

Answers will vary

93: Making Maple Syrup

sap, trunks, collect, heated, water

Last sentence: Most maple syrup comes from Canada.

94: Taking to the Skies

1. propeller
2. hot-air balloon
3. kite
4. jet

95: How the Teddy Got Its Name

Roosevelt, hunting, bear, toy, teddy

96: Why Do We Sweat?

1. Before – After
2. Lastly – First
3. After – Before
4. First – Finally

97: Predicting the Weather

pressure drops – storms

pressure raises – sunny weather

morning fog – sunny weather later

98: Salt Dough Sculptures

Pour in salt and flour – before – pouring in water

Pour in water – then – stir

Sculpt – then – bake

Paint – after - baking

99: From Cotton Fields to Fabric

dye, cotton boll, textile mill

100: A Close Look at Mushrooms

1. Circle the spores.
2. Draw an arrow to the gills.
3. Draw a box around the mycelium.
4. Draw a star by the stem.

101: Power for the Future

1. false
2. false
3. true
4. true

102: Ice Age Giants

1. canine teeth (blue)
2. megafauna (yellow)
3. glacier (red)
4. Smilodon (green)

103: Why Zoos Matter

F, O, F, O, F, F

104: Homework Problems

1. eliminated
2. tired
3. family
4. stress
5. agree or disagree depending on the reader's opinion

105: Kids and Screen Time

Answers will vary

106: Plastic Bag Ban

1. in common
2. plastic
3. reusable
4. reusable
5. in common
6. plastic

107: Too Much Testing

1. arts
2. test taking
3. anxiety
4. money

108: Computers in the Classroom

1. small – big
2. encyclopedia – Internet
3. slower – faster
4. state – globe

109: Designing Smarter Cities

Pictures will vary

110: Look for the Relationship

1. problem/solution
2. compare/contrast
3. sequence
4. cause/effect

Skills Index and Common Core Correlations

RL 3.1: Ask and answer questions to demonstrate understanding of a text, referring explicitly to the text as the basis for the answers.

Activity 1: Lost and Found

Activity 2: What Red Said

Activity 3: A Shared Lunch

Activity 4: A Racket on the Tennis Court

Activity 5: After the Rain

Activity 38: Oh, Deer!

Activity 39: A Good Start

Activity 40: The True Story of Cinderella

Activity 41: Taking Care of Alyssa

Activity 42: Hurry Up, Henry!

Activity 75: The Free Bike

Activity 76: The Day I Became a Trapeze Artist

Activity 77: No Running in the Hall

Activity 78: Thomas's Talent

RL 3.2: Recount stories, including fables, folktales, and myths from diverse cultures; determine the central message, lesson, or moral and explain how it is conveyed through key details in the text.

Activity 6: The Bossy Rooster: A Cuban Folktale

Activity 7: Frog's Escape

Activity 8: Curtis's Cupcake

Activity 9: Waking Up Walter

Activity 10: High-Flying Ida

Activity 43: The Clever Beetle

Activity 44: Theseus and the Minotaur: A Myth

Activity 45: Paul's Report

Activity 46: Jada's Paint Box

Activity 79: The Armadillo Prince

Activity 80: The Magic Ring

Activity 81: Stone Soup: A Folktale

RL 3.3: Describe characters in a story (e.g., their traits, motivations, or feelings) and explain how their actions contribute to the sequence of events

Activity 11: Perry's Surprise Disguise

Activity 12: Evelyn's Answer

Activity 13: Penguin Plunge

Activity 14: Injury and Inspiration

Activity 15: Yikes! Spiders!

Activity 47: Julius and the Dragon: Part 1

Activity 48: Julius and the Dragon: Part 2

Activity 49: The Cleanest Pig

Activity 50: Gifts from Grandma

RL 3.4: Determine the meaning of words and phrases as they are used in a text, distinguishing literal from nonliteral language.

Activity 51: Henrietta's Turn Around

Activity 52: The Spring Carnival

Activity 53: David's Big Idea

Activity 54: The Wind's Way

Activity 55: Make a Metaphor

RL 3.5: Refer to parts of stories, dramas, and poems when writing or speaking about a text, using terms such as chapter, scene, and stanza; describe how each successive part builds on earlier sections.

Activity 82: Mila and Lucy's Sleepover

Activity 83: Cheering for Andre

Activity 84: Breakfast

Activity 85: In Search of a Campsite: Act 1

Activity 86: In Search of a Campsite: Act 2

RL 3.6: Distinguish their own point of view from that of the narrator or those of the characters.

Activity 87: The Kitchen Table Mystery

Activity 88: The Party at the Park

Activity 89: The Drum: A Folktale from India

RL 3.7: Explain how specific aspects of a text's illustrations contribute to what is conveyed by the words in a story (e.g., create mood, emphasize aspects of a character or setting)

Activity 16: A New Home for Alvin

Activity 17: Help in the Storm

Activity 18: Spring Break Plans

Activity 19: Kelton's Experiment

RL 3.8: Not applicable

RL 3.9: Compare and contrast the themes, settings, and plots of stories written by the same author about the same or similar characters (e.g., in books from a series)

Activity 56: Super Fly: Setting

Activity 57: Super Fly: Plot

Activity 58: Super Fly: Theme

RI 3.1: Ask and answer questions to demonstrate understanding of a text, referring explicitly to the text as the basis for the answers.

Activity 20: Walking on the Moon

Activity 21: How the Hippo Got Its Name

Activity 22: Celebrating Holi

Activity 23: Rock Art

Activity 24: From Seed to Christmas Tree

Activity 59: Nest-Building Animals

Activity 60: Lady Liberty

Activity 61: How Hibernation Works

Activity 62: Seeds on the Move

Activity 63: All About Joints

Activity 90: An Unlikely Team

Activity 91: A Mountaintop City

Activity 92: Clowns of the Sea

Activity 93: Making Maple Syrup

RI 3.2: Determine the main idea of a text; recount the key details and explain how they support the main idea.

Activity 64: Coast-to-Coast Railroads

Activity 65: Bridges That Hang

Activity 66: Why Do We Use Soap?

Activity 67: Earthworm Work

RI 3.3: Describe the relationship between a series of historical events, scientific ideas or concepts, or steps in technical procedures in a text, using language that pertains to time, sequence, and cause/effect.

Activity 94: Taking to the Skies

Activity 95: How the Teddy Got Its Name

Activity 96: Why Do We Sweat?

Activity 97: Predicting the Weather

Activity 98: Salt Dough Sculptures

RI 3.4: Determine the meaning of general academic and domain-specific words and phrases in a text relevant to a grade 3 topic or subject area.

Activity 99: From Cotton Fields to Fabric

Activity 100: A Close Look at Mushrooms

Activity 101: Power for the Future

Activity 102: Ice Age Giants

RI 3.5: Use text features and search tools (e.g., key words, sidebars, hyperlinks) to locate information relevant to a given topic efficiently.

Activity 25: The Lives of Camels

Activity 26: Taking a Camping Trip

Activity 27: Rescuing Baby Elephants

Activity 28: The Rise of the Roller Coaster

Activity 68: The Great Barrier Reef

Activity 69: Cookbook Index

Activity 70: How Loud Is Too Loud?

RI 3.6: Distinguish their own point of view from that of the author of a text.

Activity 103: Why Zoos Matter

Activity 104: Homework Problems

Activity 105: Kids and Screen Time

RI 3.7: Use information gained from illustrations (e.g., maps, photographs) and the words in a text to demonstrate understanding of the text (e.g., where, when, why, and how key events occur).

Activity 29: Becoming a Butterfly

Activity 30: How to Draw a Bird

Activity 31: A Museum Trip

Activity 32: Animal Long Jumpers

Activity 33: Chuck What?

RI 3.8: Describe the logical connection between particular sentences and paragraphs in a text (e.g., comparison, cause/effect, first/second/third in a sequence).

Activity 106: Plastic Bag Ban

Activity 107: Too Much Testing

Activity 108: Computers in the Classroom

Activity 109: Designing Smarter Cities

Activity 110: Look for the Relationship

RI 3.9: Compare and contrast the most important points and key details presented in two texts on the same topic.

Activity 71: What Happened to the Dinosaurs?

Activity 72: Measuring Mountains

Activity 73: The Case For and Against Gym Class

Activity 74: Pondering Plastic

The following activities draw on well-known teaching and learning practices but do not include a skill listed in the Skills Index and Common Core Correlations.

Activate prior knowledge

Activity 34: Working as a Veterinarian

Activity 35: Rocks: From Solid to Liquid

Making connections to self and the world

Activity 36: Why We Sleep

Activity 37: From Old Paper to New

About the Author

Hannah Braun writes curriculum for teachers and parents of elementary-aged children. She spent eight years as a classroom teacher and has two children of her own. Hannah loves to bring about "A-ha!" moments for kids by breaking down tricky concepts into digestible parts. She holds a bachelor's degree in elementary education and a master's degree in early childhood education. Hannah is the author of the blog The Classroom Key (TheClassroomKey.com) where she shares ideas and information about best practices in teaching. In her free time, Hannah enjoys playing French horn in community bands, painting, and fitness classes. Follow her on Facebook and Instagram, both @TheClassroomKey.

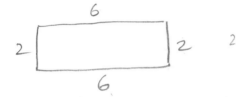

2